1

Air Quality Observation Systems in the United States

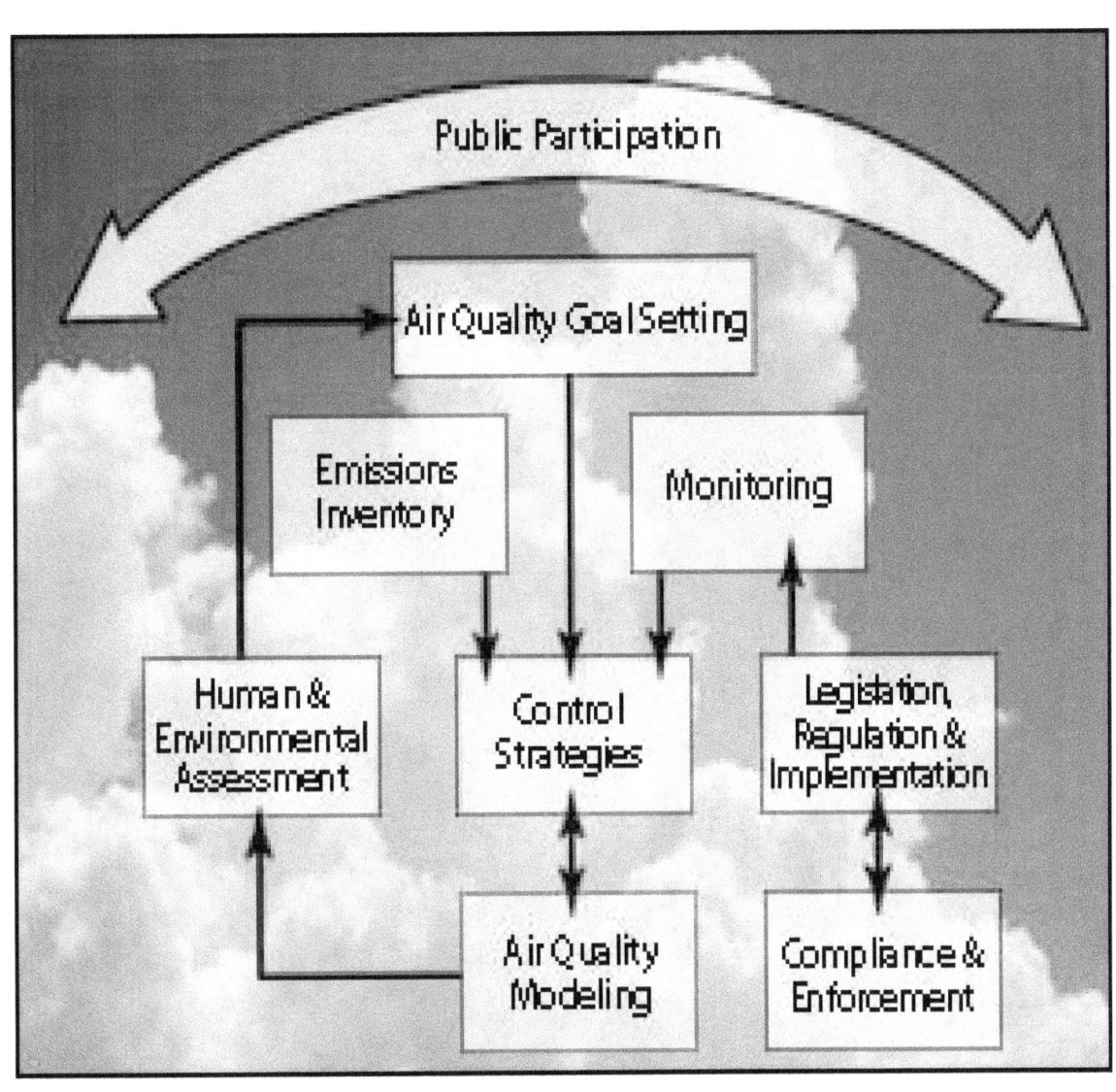

Table of Contents

Executive Summary – Air Quality Observation Systems in the United States

In June 2013, President Obama released his Climate Action Plan. The Plan calls for a range of activities to help mitigate the impacts of carbon pollution, prepare for and adapt to those impacts that cannot be avoided, and enhance international efforts to reduce the harmful global effects of climate change. Success in each of the Plan's three components will require access to and application of the highest quality atmospheric science.

Fortunately, as a result of decades of attention to the issue of air quality generally – from ozone and carbon dioxide to soot and other particulates – the United States is in good position to address the added observational and modeling challenges posed by climate change. Federal agencies and state and local partners invest hundreds of millions of dollars annually to maintain and operate the Nation's ground- and space-based air quality observation networks, and to conduct short-term field studies relating to air quality. The data collected by these activities have been indispensable to the effective development and implementation of policies to protect public health and the environment, and will be even more so as the Nation addresses the emerging impacts of climate change.

This report catalogs the wide range of U.S. air quality measurement modalities and programs, including routine regulatory and deposition networks, intensive field studies, satellites, and fixed-site special-purpose networks operated or overseen by Federal departments and agencies – including the Environmental Protection Agency (EPA), National Oceanic and Atmospheric Administration (NOAA), National Aeronautics and Space Administration (NASA), U.S. Department of Agriculture (USDA), Department of Energy (DOE), Department of Health and Human Services (DHHS), Department of Homeland Security (DHS), and Department of the Interior (DOI) – and by various state, local and tribal partners. It also highlights some leading observational needs and opportunities, and identifies some of the barriers to fulfilling those needs and leveraging those opportunities. Specific programs and the pollutants they measure are documented in detail in the appendices. Among this report's findings (not ranked in priority order) are:

Observational Needs

1. Although local and regional observation and emissions reduction efforts are generally well advanced in the United States, there is a need to improve characterization of pollutants from distant/international sources to better evaluate their contribution to domestic air quality.
2. There is a need for enhanced atmospheric, deposition, and effects monitoring to understand deposition impacts on aquatic and terrestrial ecosystems.
3. There is a growing need to document global changes in climate that have the potential to affect the natural release or atmospheric processing of pollutants.
4. There is a need for greater attention to precursors of ozone and particulate matter in order to accurately assess the success of emissions control strategies.

5. There is an ongoing need for more cost effective means of compliance monitoring, to reduce financial burdens on state and local governments.
6. There is a need for vertically resolved observations of ozone, particulate matter (including its composition), and their precursors, to evaluate and improve air quality modeling.

Opportunities

1. Satellite sensing of air quality and emissions is rapidly maturing in its capability to augment and extend the spatial and temporal coverage offered by fixed-site monitoring networks and short-term special studies, allowing for unprecedented, high value ventures into satellite-based, ecosystem-characteristic measurements. U.S. agency geostationary missions in the near future will provide coverage at scales highly relevant to urban air quality, presenting notable future opportunities for analysis and integration.
2. Air quality models are increasingly able to reliably augment direct observations with credible spatial, temporal, and compositional information lacking in direct measurements.
3. Open access policies are providing enhanced access to observational data, metadata, and processing tools, facilitating harmonization and consolidation of disparate datasets and collaboration among previously unrelated research teams.

Barriers to Progress

1. Funding for long-term maintenance and updates of observation infrastructure is often subject to annual budgeting processes that inhibit long-range planning.
2. Agencies often support their own priority programs rather than pooling resources on joint efforts in domains of shared responsibility.
3. Some issues are not adequately addressed because they do not fall clearly within any one entity's regulatory purview.
4. Funding is often focused on the development of advanced technologies without adequate accompanying support for the development of tools for processing and transferring the resulting data streams.
5. In the absence of government mandates or other incentives, commercialization of air quality monitoring technologies suffers from weak market incentives.

Conclusion

The United States has a robust and invaluable network of air quality observation systems, and recent improvements in technology are providing unprecedented opportunities to enhance current capabilities. However, current funding patterns and limited coordination among departments and agencies with equities in air quality observations are preventing the Nation from reaching its full potential in this important domain.

The NSTC Committee on Environment, Natural Resources, and Sustainability (CENRS) should consider establishing a standing, multi-agency Observations Working Group under the Air Quality Research Subcommittee (AQRS) whose responsibilities could include:

a. conducting periodic adequacy reviews of the Nation's air quality observational capabilities;
b. identifying and addressing gaps and overlaps among programs;
c. building cooperation and coordination among government programs;
d. advising on minimum standards for program design/implementation;
e. promoting the use of common data formats and communications protocols;
f. identifying opportunities for development of, and review/recommending the use of, new observational technology;
g. fostering data quality elements, monitoring across appropriate gradients, and the role of modeling;
h. identifying low-priority networks that can be discontinued and defunded in order to offset the costs of new investments.

The Working Group could also develop strategies to address such needs as:

a. initiating monitoring of reactive gas and particulate nitrogen compounds, which are precursors of ozone and particulate matter, contributors to acid deposition, and nutrients in ecosystems;
b. collocating instrumentation at core measurement sites to facilitate inter-comparison with satellite observations;
c. targeting observations in rural/remote areas to measure regional backgrounds and contributions from long-range transport of pollutants;
d. establishing more robust air toxics monitoring near major industrial facilities to help investigate whether air toxics emissions are associated with reported human health effects in nearby communities; and
e. targeting intensive field studies designed to elucidate critical processes that determine atmospheric concentrations of ozone and particulate matter and other air pollutants.

Introduction

Accurate information about air pollutants in the troposphere, such as ozone, particulates, and their respective precursors, is essential to decision-making in domains as diverse as human health, environmental protection, climate change, and agriculture, as well as for assessments of air quality management strategies and policies. Atmospheric observations have only grown in importance as the risks posed by global climate change have come more clearly into focus, and observations will be critical in the years ahead both for tracking the impacts of mitigation strategies and predicting national needs in the realm of adaptation and preparedness.

Modeling of the emissions and processes that affect air quality is improving rapidly. But direct observation remains the gold standard for tracking man-made and naturally occurring atmospheric species, the spatial and temporal distribution of which are governed by such complex influences as: the sources of those species; relevant meteorology; physical and chemical processes that transport, transform, and remove various species; and exchanges between the atmosphere and terrestrial and aquatic environs.

Reliable assessments of atmospheric composition are especially important given the high financial stakes; the costs and benefits of Clean Air Act requirements alone are estimated to be on the order of tens of billions of dollars per year (National Research Council, 2004). In response to such regulatory and other incentives, a wide variety of Federal agencies and organizations make air quality observations or process or take advantage of air quality data, including EPA, NOAA, NASA, USDA, DOE, DHHS, DHS, and DOI, as do associated state, local and tribal partners. In many cases, these agencies share common information needs, and the value of air quality observations could be enhanced by coordinated planning or shared operations. Opportunities also exist to increase the value of air quality observations by integrating them across environmental media, pollutant categories, and spatial scales.

This report (1) describes the measurement parameters, locations, and sponsoring organizations of ambient monitoring and other air quality observation and assessment efforts, focusing primarily on U.S. assets; and (2) identifies observational gaps and opportunities to enhance the value of existing measurement programs through inter-agency cooperation and collaboration. Appendices provide a comprehensive inventory of monitoring networks, observation programs, and pollutants measured.

Current and Emerging Air Quality Assessment Challenges

Over the last two decades, air quality management in the United States has focused on regional-scale air pollutants such as ozone, particulate matter, and acid deposition, all of which remain issues of concern and are likely to continue as such for the foreseeable future, especially if air quality standards continue to tighten.

Traditional management strategies typically involve independent, specific approaches based on targeted monitoring of individual pollutants. Increasingly, however, air quality management requires a more comprehensive and well-integrated assessment framework:

- Multiple pollutants – Typically, multiple pollutants are emitted by individual emission sources and participate in interrelated atmospheric, chemical, and physical transformation and loss processes. Too often, however, measurement systems are still structured to support only single-pollutant assessments.
- Multiple environmental media – The atmosphere is closely coupled with terrestrial and aquatic systems. These systems are major sinks for air pollutants, leading to effects on ecosystems from acids, nutrients, and toxics. In turn, soils, vegetation, and aquatic systems re-emit mercury and persistent organic pollutants (POPs), and meteorology and climate affect biogenic and biomass burning emissions. These linkages require a broader perspective on environmental monitoring, which traditionally addresses issues on an isolated, single-media basis. Coordinated monitoring across multiple media is required to accurately assess progress mitigating the effects of atmospheric pollution on human health, ecosystems, and agriculture.
- Multiple spatial scales – Long-range (inter-regional and intercontinental) pollutant transport is becoming increasingly important as transport across U.S. borders increases from expanded world development and as local emissions decline (NRC, 2009a). Meanwhile, urban-based field studies have demonstrated high pollutant levels in the near-source/roadway environment, where a majority of the North American population lives and the chemical environment is dynamic and poorly understood. These scale issues, at opposite ends of the spatial spectrum, challenge the current assessment framework that emphasizes regional air quality management.
- Climate-air quality interactions – The bi-directional interaction between air quality and climate change impacts air quality management. A variety of emissions, atmospheric chemistry, and transport processes that affect air quality are modified by climate change. Conversely, several air pollutants, particularly greenhouse gases, ozone, and black carbon particulate matter, are significant climate forcers, and air quality changes impact atmospheric and emissions processes, impacting climate. Moreover, climate forcers and conventional air pollutants are largely emitted from common sources. Consequently, emerging energy policies designed for moderating climate and policies designed to improve air quality are intrinsically connected, and measurement-system design should reflect this relationship.

Addressing these challenges would also address several challenges highlighted in integrated observational strategies (see Appendix A) and in three reports by the National Academies.

In *Global Sources of Local Pollution: An Assessment of Long-Range Transport of Key Air Pollutants to and from the United States* (NRC, 2009a), improved satellite observations, in situ monitoring, and intensive field campaigns were all highlighted as ways to improve understanding of air pollution transport. In *Air Quality Management in the United States* (NRC, 2004), the highest priority recommendation for improving air quality management was to "strengthen the scientific and technical capacity of the [air quality management] system to assess risk and track progress." Carefully designed and maintained monitoring can contribute to this progress by improving understanding of ambient concentrations, emissions, transport, and deposition and by improving modeling through more complete data for model evaluation.

A third National Academies report, *Observing Weather and Climate from the Ground Up: A Nationwide Network of Networks* (NRC, 2009b), cited four types of observations as the "highest priority observations needed to address current inadequacies," all of which are relevant for air quality monitoring:

- Height of the planetary boundary layer
- Soil moisture and temperature profiles
- High-resolution vertical profiles of humidity
- Measurements of air quality and related chemical composition above the surface layer.

Uses of Air Quality Observations

The air quality observation systems discussed in this report serve four broad disciplines: (1) human exposure and health effects, (2) ecosystem exposure and effects, (3) air quality management efforts, and (4) basic atmospheric science, including linkages between air quality and climate change. Although disciplines (1) and (2) are described in general terms below, this report does not attempt to elucidate the major needs or gaps of U.S. observation programs focused specifically on human exposure and health effects or ecosystem impacts—including studies of physical or chemical properties of aquatic and terrestrial systems—which generally need especially high-resolution data over multiple observational axes.

Human Exposure and Health Effects

Relating health effects to observed concentrations of pollutants is a critical use of air quality observations. Forecasting of future air quality conditions allows the general public, particularly sensitive groups, to modify behavior and protect their health by reducing potential exposure to poor air quality. Verification and improvement of model predictions and interpretative forecasts relies on timely availability of accurate and precise observations. In addition to surface observations of criteria pollutants, such as ozone and particulate matter, measurements of their precursors, particulate matter composition, and the vertical distribution of pollutants are needed to improve model predictions.

Many epidemiological studies of the health effects of air pollution use data from existing monitoring networks. For example, Pope et al. (2009) used measurements from EPA monitoring networks to show that decreases in $PM_{2.5}$ concentrations lead to increased life expectancy. In general, however, the use of existing monitoring networks for epidemiological studies of air pollution poses challenges. Monitoring networks typically involve air quality observations from relatively small numbers of instruments in metropolitan areas, placed in areas that may not capture the full range of concentrations to which people within the area are exposed. Likewise, monitoring networks of criteria pollutants are designed to provide pollutant levels over an averaging time defined by the National Ambient Air Quality Standards (NAAQS), which can prove limiting for some health studies.

For measurements not directly related to compliance with air quality standards, such as air toxics or speciation of particulate matter, the frequency of measurements can be considerably lower than ideal for epidemiological studies.
Further, when data from an existing monitoring network are used to study health effects, the research is limited to the chemical species being measured by the network, as well as by pre-determined measurement periods and spatial coverage.

It is important to note that health impacts are the primary inputs into the evolution of NAAQS, which in turn influence monitoring design. Other types of health impacts research (e.g., for air toxics) complement the epidemiological studies that use ambient monitors, but the inter-relationship of the monitoring design and health effects studies illustrates the need for careful design of ambient monitoring programs. This network design should generally consider the same scale (e.g., local, regional) as the epidemiology studies used to set the health-based standards.

Ecosystem Exposure and Effects

Atmospheric observations are a major part of ecological effects assessment efforts, either directly or through air quality models. Watershed acidification, eutrophication, and direct damage to vegetation are examples of major ecosystem welfare issues whose understanding can be enhanced by atmospheric characterization studies. The ecosystem assessment community is an important client of air quality observations, using available data as inputs to ecosystem exposure models and as trend indicators relating the effectiveness of emissions strategies on atmospheric deposition. The characterization demands for ecosystem analyses may be as demanding as those associated with human health and exposure communities, given the spatial heterogeneity of vegetation, soil types, and microclimates within and across watersheds and ecosystems that affect, and are affected by, atmospheric deposition. Furthermore, most U.S. monitoring stations are distributed according to population-weighted criteria, creating major information gaps in sensitive ecosystems.

Air Quality Management Efforts

Air quality management practice includes the establishment of human and ecosystem health-based standards and the subsequent development of rules, programs, and implementation steps designed to achieve the emission changes needed to meet air quality targets. The cyclic nature of air quality management reflects both the evolution of air quality standards (based on improving knowledge of the effects of air pollution) and evaluation of whether implemented programs produced intended results. In recent years, air quality management has sought more direct evidence of the connections along the source-to-effects continuum, and of the relationship between emissions changes and air quality improvements, to better assess the effectiveness of emissions strategies.

The regulatory nature of air quality management decisions places special demands on the observations used to support this work. Ambient monitoring of criteria air pollutants such as ozone, particulate matter, etc., is designed to be used to determine if an area is compliant with a specified NAAQS. Only certified measurements from Federal Reference or Equivalent Methods (FRM/FEM) can be used for comparison to the NAAQS. However, FRM/FEMs have not been established for toxic air pollutants, in part because the regulatory structure of the Clean Air Act (CAA) does not require ambient monitoring for these pollutants. In practice, the reliance on FRM/FEM certification and a lack of regulatory drivers has hindered development and commercialization of potentially useful air quality monitoring technologies.

Basic Atmospheric Science, Including Linkages between Air Quality and Climate Change

Air quality data can improve the characterization of physical and chemical processes underlying pollutant release, transformation, and removal and can inform the development, evaluation, and refinement of quantitative atmospheric chemistry models. Such models, in turn, can be critical to air quality management efforts and to assessments of air quality on health, ecosystems, and climate. And while models are essential for making predictions, such as air quality forecasts, climate predictions, and estimated impacts of future emissions changes, they are also key to characterizing the multi-dimensional (space, time, and species) chemical state of the current atmosphere and to understanding historical conditions.

Overview of Observation Programs

A variety of measurement programs support air quality assessments. These include:

- routine regulatory and deposition networks
- intensive aircraft and ground-based field studies
- radiosonde programs
- satellite measurements
- ground-based remote-sensing networks
- focused, fixed-site, special purpose networks

The following inventory of representative programs is not intended to be comprehensive but focuses on extant, routinely operating North American networks, with some mention of European and international efforts relevant to North American assessments. More detailed information is available in the appendices.

Routine Surface-Based Ambient Air and Deposition Networks

Routine ambient air and deposition monitoring networks in North America comprise more than 3000 fixed platforms (Figure 1), measuring numerous gaseous species and aerosol properties (Appendices B and C). Many of these longstanding U.S. networks were required or catalyzed by the 1970 Clean Air Act (CAA), subsequent CAA amendments, National Ambient Air Quality Standard (NAAQS) reviews, and/or National Academy of Sciences (NAS) recommendations. Examples include the Clean Air Status and Trends Network (CASTNET) and National Atmospheric Deposition Program (NADP) addressing acidification; the Photochemical Assessment Monitoring Stations (PAMS) in response to persistent ozone pollution; and the $PM_{2.5}$ monitoring networks following promulgation of the 1997 NAAQS. Federal regulations describe how sites in these networks are to be located, and the Federal Reference Methods (FRM) or Federal Equivalent Methods (FEM) for the measurements made at many of the required sites.

Most routine air quality monitoring stations in the United States are owned and operated by nearly 300 state and local government and Tribal agencies. These state and local air monitoring stations (SLAMS) are the principal source of ambient measurements of the six criteria air pollutants (ozone, nitrogen dioxide, carbon monoxide, sulfur dioxide, lead, particulate matter - PM_{10} and $PM_{2.5}$), each of which has one or more NAAQS specifying a concentration level and averaging period (http://www.epa.gov/ttn/naaqs/). Most of these networks also include stations operated by Federal agencies, typically in rural / remote sites. These networks are indirectly supported by extensive meteorological networks (Appendix D).

National air monitoring regulations for U.S. programs are codified in Parts 50, 53, and 58 of Title 40 of the Code of Federal Regulations (CFR).

Funding for these programs is through CAA Sections 103 and 105 concerning Federal grants to agencies and tribes. States and local agencies are required to match Federal Section 105 contributions.

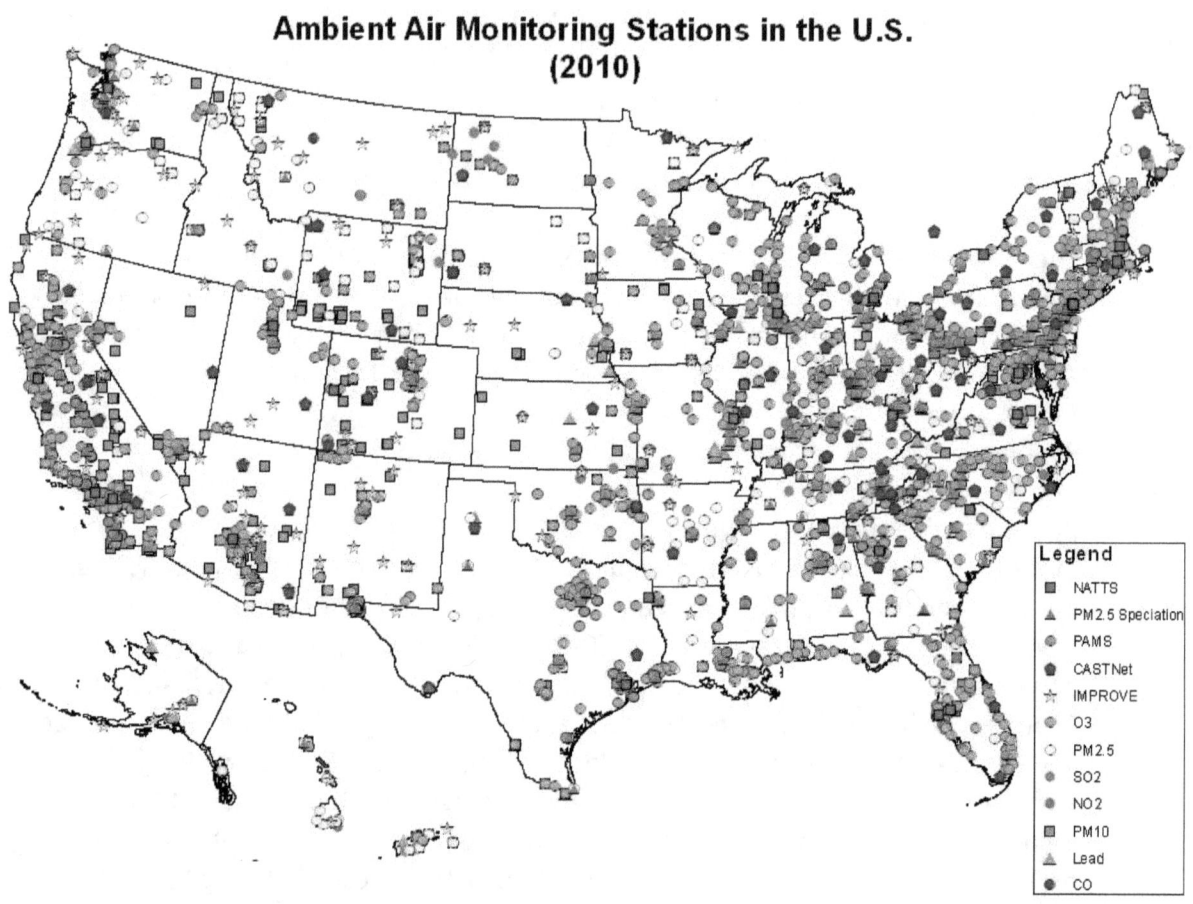

Figure 1. Aggregate map of the majority of routine U.S. monitoring stations, illustrating relatively broad coverage across the continental United States. Note spatial gaps in sparsely populated areas.

Criteria Gas and Ozone Precursor Monitoring

Criteria Gas Networks -- Approximately 1500 surface stations measure some combination of criteria gases, with nearly 1100 of these stations measuring ozone, using FRMs or FEMs. Several hundred monitors report concentrations for CO, SO_2, and NO/NOx. The majority of these stations are SLAMS, although Federal agency networks such as CASTNET, National Park Service (NPS) monitors, and a variety of special purpose monitors provide additional coverage (Appendices B and C). CASTNET and NPS provide the majority of rural criteria pollutant platforms.

Photochemical Assessment Monitoring Stations (PAMS) -- Approximately 75 sites in 22 cities were deployed by state and local agencies in the early 1990s to measure ozone precursors, largely in response to a 1991 National Academy of Sciences study (NRC, 1991). PAMS and the air toxics network (see below) provide the majority of routinely available non-methane organic carbon (NMOC) measurements. A number of ozone precursor C2-C10 alkanes and alkenes, aromatics, formaldehyde, and acetaldehyde are measured using a combination of continuous methods and sampling techniques over 3- and 24-hour collection periods, often limited to the ozone season (April – October). The 1990 CAA Amendments required areas classified as serious and above with respect to the contemporary (1990-1992) ozone NAAQS to implement PAMS, which has undergone minor modifications since then. Most volatile organic compound (VOC) sampling sites include instrumentation for O_3 and NO/NOx.

Particulate Monitoring

$PM_{2.5}$, PM_{10}, and $PM_{10-2.5}$ Mass Networks -- The 1997 promulgation of a fine particulate NAAQS (EPA, 1997) led to deployment of over 1500 $PM_{2.5}$ sites (about 1000 currently), used to determine whether an area complies with the standard. These sites use an FRM or FEM, sampling over 24 hours daily, or every third or sixth day. Nearly 300 additional measurements not meeting FRM or FEM specifications are provided by the chemical speciation sites (see below). Approximately 600 stations provide indirect measurements of continuous (hourly resolution) $PM_{2.5}$ mass, using a variety of techniques. Continuous $PM_{2.5}$ mass measurements have been granted FEM status based on revised monitoring regulations issued in 2006 (EPA, 2006) that provided new approaches for demonstrating equivalency.

Approximately 1000 PM_{10} samplers (24-hr sampling period, typically collected every sixth day) remain in operation. Although a $PM_{10-2.5}$ standard has not been promulgated, EPA developed a $PM_{10-2.5}$ FRM based on mass difference of concurrent PM_{10} and $PM_{2.5}$ measurements. $PM_{10-2.5}$ measurements are incorporated in the NCore network (see below).

Interagency Monitoring of Protected Visual Environments (IMPROVE) Program -- The IMPROVE network, with over 100 sites, has provided nearly a two-decade record of major components of $PM_{2.5}$ (sulfate, nitrate, organic and elemental carbon fractions, and trace metals) in pristine areas of the United States (Figure 2). IMPROVE is led by the National Park Service, with various other Federal and state agencies providing support operations. The primary focus of the network is to track visibility and trends in visibility.

$PM_{2.5}$ Chemical Speciation Monitoring -- In addition to the IMPROVE network, over 300 EPA speciation sites were added from the years 2000 - 2002 in urban areas of the United States to assist $PM_{2.5}$ assessment efforts. No FRM exists for particulate speciation, which is not directly required to determine attainment, and there are slight differences among the different monitors used in the Chemical Speciation Network (CSN).

However, the network's coverage (Figure 2) across urban and rural areas has proven essential for a wide range of research and analysis. The speciation networks typically collect a 24-hour sample every three, and sometimes six, days. Daily 24-hour speciation collection is limited to occasional efforts in the SEARCH (see below) network. Similarly, only a handful of sites provide near continuous speciation data, usually limited to some combination of sulfate, carbon (organic and elemental splits), and nitrate. This enables insights into diurnal speciation patterns, helpful in diagnosing various cause-effect phenomena related to emissions characterization, source attribution analysis, and model evaluation. In addition, the National Air Toxics Trends Stations (NATTS; see below) include near continuous aethalometer measurements based on optical absorption as a surrogate for absorbing aerosol (e.g., elemental carbon).

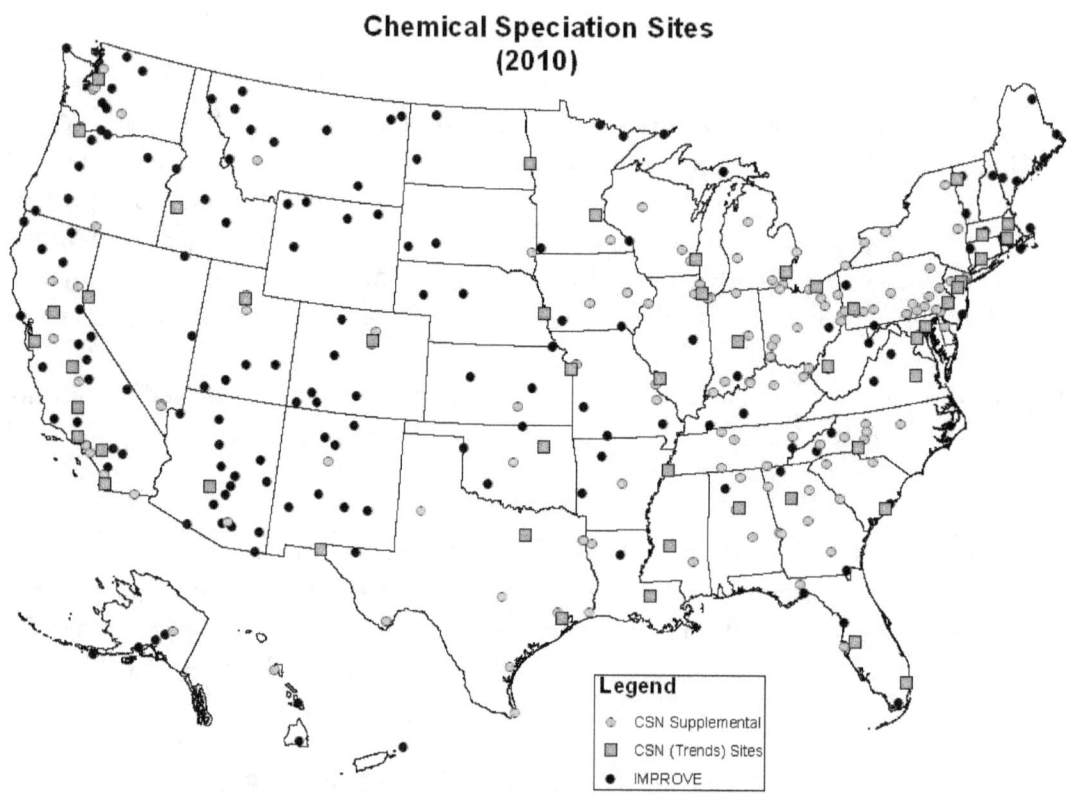

Figure 2. Locations of chemical speciation sites delineated by program type.

SouthEastern Aerosol Research and Characterization (SEARCH) Study -- SEARCH is an industry-funded network that originally emerged from the Southern Oxidants Study (SOS) in the 1990s. It has operated for over a decade in response to 1997 revisions to the NAAQS for ground-level ozone and particulate matter. SEARCH provides an array of standard criteria pollutant measurements, in addition to daily PM speciation at selected times and locations, gaseous ammonia (NH_3), total peroxyacetyl nitrate (PAN), nitric acid (HNO_3), reactive oxidized nitrogen (NOy), and true nitrogen dioxide (i.e., a measurement of NO_2 concentration unaffected by other nitrogen oxides, which contaminate FRM NO_2 measurements).

These measurements typically had not been available in major government-funded routine networks. Measurements of pollutant composition, as well as mass, are necessary in order to identify sources of ozone precursors and fine particulate matter, and to attribute health effects to specific components.

PM Supersites Program -- This program (Solomon et al., 2008) provided highly resolved aerosol measurements at eight U.S. cities for several time periods from 1999 through 2004, with some sites collecting data after 2004. A number of instrument configurations were deployed, ranging from additional locations for standard speciation monitors, to systems capturing near-continuous size-dependent speciation profiles.

The National Core (NCore) Network

NCore (Scheffe et al., 2009) is an 80-site multiple pollutant supplement to the routine monitoring networks. It was fostered by the Ambient Air Monitoring Strategy for State, Local, and Tribal Air Agencies (EPA, 2008), and promulgated in the 2006 Code of Federal Regulations as part of the new monitoring rule (EPA, 2006). NCore is designed to capture urban- and regional-scale representative concentrations of a variety of trace gases (CO, SO_2, NOy, and NO) and aerosols (PM_{10} and $PM_{2.5}$ mass and chemical speciation) to support a range of health effect, model evaluation, and other research studies. The NCore sites are designated multiple pollutant sites that require co-location with existing $PM_{2.5}$ chemical speciation measurements. Deployment of the network took place through 2011.

Air Toxics Monitoring Program

National Air Toxics Trends Stations (NATTS) Network -- State and local agencies have measured a variety of metallic and gaseous toxic air pollutants at over 200 locations since the 1980s. Broad access to and use of these data was hampered by a lack of centralized databases and multiple sampling and laboratory protocols, creating data quality and consistency concerns. To address these inconsistencies, the NATTS network was conceived in 2001, consisting of 27 sites. The sampling protocol typically has been every sixth day for 24 hours.

Among the priority ranked 33 air toxics of U.S. concern, observations of benzene and other common aromatics are generally widespread and relatively reliable. However, other potentially important air toxics are less well represented in air monitoring. During the initial start-up of the NATTS, six priority pollutants (formaldehyde, benzene, 1,3-butadiene, hexavalent chromium, acrolein, and arsenic) were targeted for inclusion, based on results of the 1996 National Air Toxics Assessment (NATA; http://www.epa.gov/ttn/atw/natamain/index.html).

Building on efficiencies in methodologies and the 1999 and 2002 NATAs, NATTS observations expanded to include the following:

- Gas-phase compounds: acetaldehyde, acrolein, benzene, carbon tetrachloride, chloroform, dichloropropane, dichloromethane, formaldehyde, naphthalene, perchloroethylene, trichloroethylene, vinyl chloride, and 1,3-butadiene.
- Metals in PM_{10}: nickel, arsenic, cadmium, manganese, beryllium, and lead.
- Total suspended particle (TSP) mass: hexavalent chromium.
- Combined gas-phase and TSP: naphthalene and benzo(a)pyrene.
- Light absorbing carbon through aethalometers at a subset of sites.

In 2009, the EPA initiated a school air toxics study (http://www.epa.gov/schoolair/) to sample and analyze for a variety of hazardous air pollutants (HAPs; "air toxics") at 63 schools in 22 states. The Integrated Atmospheric Deposition Network (IADN) program (see below) also analyzes for selected metals (As, Pb, Cd, and Se) and other air toxics, while the National Atmospheric Deposition Program (NADP) includes mercury (Hg) monitoring in some sites. These programs are discussed below. The spatial and temporal patterns of many HAPs have strong localized signals associated with near field source emissions.

This makes characterization of air toxics concentrations especially challenging, given both the number of chemical species of concern and the difficulty in accounting for impacts of a myriad of emission sources. Consequently, the U.S. EPA has primarily relied on air quality modeling to communicate risks associated with air toxics in the NATA reports.

Deposition Networks

Precipitation-Based Networks: NADP and IADN -- Precipitation chemistry is an important link between the atmosphere and terrestrial and aquatic systems. The National Atmospheric Deposition Program (NADP) currently consists of five subnetworks. Two of these subnetworks, the National Trends Network (NTN) and the Atmospheric Integrated Research Monitoring Network (AIRMoN), oversee approximately 250 sites that analyze for ions that have significant acidification and eutrophication effects. AIRMoN provides precipitation samples that facilitate temporal resolution. NTN data have described trends in precipitation chemistry across the United States since about 1978.

Two additional NADP subnetworks measure mercury. The Mercury Deposition Network (MDN) includes over 90 sites that measure total mercury in precipitation. The Atmospheric Mercury Network (AMNet) provides data on the atmospheric concentrations of mercury in gaseous and particulate forms, and other data needed to estimate dry deposition at twenty sites across North America. Monitoring mercury in the atmosphere is important for model evaluation and tracking the atmospheric response to emissions reductions.

AMNet, which began as a pilot partnership networking and standardizing previously deployed instruments, was formally adopted by NADP in 2009. The joint Canadian-United States Integrated Atmospheric Deposition Network (IADN) includes a mix of stations across the Great Lakes that sample both precipitation and ambient air for a range of toxic compounds. IADN emphasizes measurement of many of the more persistent organic compounds, including polychlorinated biphenyls (PCBs), pesticides, dioxins, and toxic metals (lead, cadmium, arsenic, and selenium).

Clean Air Status and Trends Network (CASTNET) -- CASTNET was established in the early 1990s to track changes in dry deposition of major inorganic ions (nitrate and sulfate) and gaseous precursors associated with CAA Title 4 reductions in sulfur and nitrogen, designed to address surface water acidification in eastern North America. The network of over 80 sites has expanded from an eastern United States focus to cover large areas in the West. CASTNET provides weekly averaged ambient measurements of major ions (sulfate, nitrate, and ammonium) and gaseous sulfur dioxide and nitric acid. A subset of sites includes ozone and IMPROVE $PM_{2.5}$ speciation instruments. CASTNET site locations were designed to reflect regional scale air mass samples, relatively free from local urban source signals. The ambient concentrations are used in algorithms that estimate deposition velocity to calculate dry deposition.

The Ammonia Monitoring Network (AMoN) is the only network providing a consistent, long-term record of ammonia gas concentrations across the United States. AMoN is an approved NADP network and uses passive samplers collecting weekly integrated measurements, located at nearly 50 of the CASTNET locations.

Other Air Monitoring Networks

For completeness, European air monitoring networks and national/international networks for monitoring persistent organic pollutants (POPs) are listed respectively in Appendices E and F.

Accessing Surface Network Data

Access to routine measurements is available through the following portals:
- EPA's Air Quality System (http://www.epa.gov/ttn/airs/airsaqs/) and related DataMart (http://www.epa.gov/ttn/airs/aqsdatamart/) house criteria gas, PAMS, PM mass, PM speciation, and air toxics data.
- EPA's AIRNow (http://www.airnow.gov/) and AIRNowTech (http://www.airnowtech.org/) provide near real time access to ozone and continuous $PM_{2.5}$ mass data.
- VIEWS (Visualization Information Exchange Web System - http://vista.cira.colostate.edu/views/ developed by the Regional Planning Organizations (RPOs) in support of visibility assessments) houses IMPROVE and EPA $PM_{2.5}$ speciation data.

- CASTNET (http://www.epa.gov/castnet/), NADP (http://nadp.sws.uiuc.edu/), and IADN (http://www.epa.gov/glnpo/monitoring/air2/index.html) provide direct access to deposition data. NADP data includes sub-networks (NTN, MDN, AMNet, AMoN) and AIRMoN (http://nadp.sws.uiuc.edu/airmon/).
- The Health Effects Institute (HEI) air quality database provides access to, and analysis tools for, processed $PM_{2.5}$ chemical speciation data (http://www.healtheffects.org/research.htm).
- Supersites Integrated Relational Database (SIRD) is described at http://www.epa.gov/ttn/amtic/ssdatamg.html.
- SouthEastern Aerosol Research and CHaracterization (SEARCH) is described and data availability identified at http://www.atmospheric-research.com/studies/SEARCH/index.html.
- Interagency Real-Time Smoke Particulate Monitoring provides real-time smoke concentration data (along with other meteorological information) from portable smoke monitors, and is described at http://app.airsis.com/USFS/.

Intensive Field Campaigns

Intensive field campaigns (Appendix G) of relatively short duration supplement routine long term monitoring networks by measuring spatial, temporal, and compositional distribution of pollutants and precursors.

These studies are designed to investigate the emission and physical and chemical processing of precursors and pollutants to understand their source, fate, transport, and removal. Typically, field campaigns use some combination of aircraft- and/or ship-based studies, satellite- and ground-based remote sensing, research-grade instrumentation, and advanced analytical methods. These efforts complement routine ground-based measurements, which usually do not address reactive gaseous species, aerosol size distributions, organic chemistry characterization, and vertically stratified data.

There is a long history of intensive field campaigns, starting with the Regional Air Pollution Study (RAPS) in the 1970s which formed the basis for evaluating the early photochemical models used in ozone assessments. Landmark campaigns in the United States through the 1980s and 1990s were reviewed as part of the 2000 NARSTO ozone assessment (Solomon et al, 2000), including the Southern California Air Quality Study, the San Joaquin Valley Air Quality Study (SJAQS)/Atmospheric Utility Signatures, Predictions, and EXperiments (AUSPEX), and the Southern Oxidant Study (SOS). Over the last decade, there has been a series of field campaigns focusing on characterization of surface-level aerosols through the PM Supersites program (Solomon et al., 2008).

While early campaigns focused on urban environments, the Eulerian Model Evaluation Field Study (EMEFS) and SOS during the early 1990s shifted the focus toward regional spatial scales. This was consistent with the dominant air pollution concerns of the time, notably acid rain and ozone.

In addition to addressing urban areas of concern, such as Houston and Los Angeles, more recent campaigns have extended spatial scales beyond regional studies to address long-range transport and continental-scale atmospheric processes. Some of these campaigns include local and regional studies for the northeast and southeast United States, portions of Texas, and central and southern California, and intercontinental studies of transport across North America and the Atlantic, Pacific, and Indian Oceans. A variety of Federal agencies (particularly NOAA and NASA) and state entities have served as leads for these studies. Appendix G provides a listing of key studies conducted since the late 1990s, with important earlier campaigns identified in footnotes. Several recent, highly relevant, campaigns are briefly described below.

The Intercontinental Transport and Chemical Transformations project of 2002 (ITCT-2k2) investigated springtime transport along the Pacific coast of North America. The campaign combined ground- and aircraft-based measurements with model simulations and satellite data products. The focus was on tropospheric chemistry and transport of ozone, fine particles, and chemically-active greenhouse compounds. The study shed light on the intercontinental transport of ozone and aerosols, and the impacts this transport has on local air quality and climate.

In 2004, the International Consortium for Atmospheric Research on Transport and Transformation (ICARTT) served as an organizing umbrella for North American and European field campaigns addressing regional scale processes in both continents, as well as trans-Atlantic transport phenomena (Fehsenfeld et al., 2006). The North American studies included the Intercontinental Chemical Transport Experiment - North America (INTEX-NA 2004) and the New England Air Quality Study - Intercontinental Transport and Chemical Transformation (NEAQS – ITCT 2004) programs. Analysis was based on a variety of satellite, aircraft, ship-based, and ground-based measurements. The ICARTT campaigns provided insights into trans-Atlantic processing of ozone precursors, lightning-generated NO_x emissions, secondary organic aerosol processes, and biomass burning.

The ICARTT campaigns had been preceded by the North American Regional Experiment (NARE) in the 1990s, which studied synoptic scale transport in the North Atlantic (Fehsenfeld et al., 1996; Penkett et al., 1998). The Transport and Chemical Evolution over the Pacific (TRACE-P) campaign of 2001 catalyzed much of our current understanding of Asian outflow to North America. The INTEX-NA mission was followed by the 2006 Intercontinental Chemical Transport Experiment (Phase B) (INTEX-B) aircraft mission, which studied pollutant transport flow across the north Pacific and into the western United States. INTEX-B was also linked with the 2006 Megacity Initiative: Local and Global Research Observations (MILAGRO) mission, which studied pollutant outflow from Mexico City. Most of the large intercontinental scale field campaigns are considered key parts of the IGAC program (Appendix A). Findings specific to Northern Hemisphere transport have been synthesized by the Hemispheric Transport of Air Pollution (HTAP) task force (Keating and Zuber, 2007).

The Texas Air Quality Study (TexAQS and TexAQS II) during 2000 and 2006 involved intensive research campaigns designed to address some of the unique VOC chemistry and transport features of southeastern Texas. The 2006 program extended the earlier study to address climate-air quality linkages and probe nighttime NOx and NOy chemistry.

The Bay Region Atmospheric Chemistry Experiment (BRACE) was conceived in response to persistent increasing trends of nitrogen oxide emissions in Florida, in order to assess potential effects on air quality and the ecological health of Tampa Bay and its surroundings. BRACE began in 2000 and has included both long-term and short-term intensive measurement campaigns, focusing on assessment of atmospheric nitrogen deposition to Tampa Bay. This program helped develop modeling approaches for numerous eastern U.S. estuaries, and has been augmented by additional field campaigns elsewhere, most notably in eastern North Carolina. Key participants included the Florida Department of Environmental Protection, Tampa Bay Electric Company, EPA, NOAA, Argonne National Laboratory, numerous universities, and several additional Florida state agencies.

The PM Supersites program complemented routine $PM_{2.5}$ monitoring by deploying research instrumentation in intensive field campaigns to obtain highly time-resolved data on multiple aerosol physical and chemical properties in major U.S. cities (Atlanta, Baltimore, Fresno, Houston, Los Angeles, Pittsburgh, St. Louis, and New York).

These data sets, spanning portions of 1999 – 2004 with some sites operating in later years, addressed three primary objectives: development of monitoring methods and transfer to operational agencies; support for health effects research; and State Implementation Plan (SIP) development. Several findings are synthesized in dedicated special journal issues (Pandis et al., 2005; Geller and Solomon, 2006; Solomon et al., 2008).

The Los Angeles Supersite and the Southern California Particle Matter Center spawned interest in near-roadway characterizations by providing measurements of particles near highways, particularly ultrafine particle numbers. This work showed very high particle concentrations near the highway (Zhu et al., 2002), with concentrations decreasing and size distributions changing with increased distance from the roadway. Near-roadway studies have since been undertaken, primarily by EPA, in several other cities, including Detroit, Raleigh, and Las Vegas. Near-roadway measurements and studies provide an important bridge between atmospheric and health sciences, given the combination of highly variable pollutant concentrations in populated locations. The EPA is developing technical requirements for monitoring to improve the understanding of exposures in near roadway environments.

The Polar Study using Aircraft, Remote Sensing, Surface Measurements and Models of Climate Chemistry, Aerosols, and Transport (POLARCAT) was a coordinated international series of field studies conducted as part of the International Polar Year 2007-2008 (IPY).

Under this activity, NASA led the 2008 Arctic Research of the Composition of the Troposphere from Aircraft and Satellites (ARCTAS) project, largely based in Canada. This field study addressed a variety of issues impacting the Arctic atmosphere, including Eurasian and North American fires, halogen chemistry, light absorbing carbon, and persistent pollutants. Prior to ARCTAS deployment in Canada, NASA had conducted a series of flights with scientists from the California Air Resources Board (CARB). These flights, already configured for the ARCTAS mission, examined California's atmosphere to better understand the chemical dynamics of smog and greenhouse gases over the state.

NOAA also led two field studies as part of the IPY: Aerosol, Radiation, and Cloud Processes affecting Arctic Climate (ARCPAC) and International Chemistry Experiment in the Arctic LOwer Troposphere (ICEALOT). ARCPAC involved the deployment of the NOAA WP-3D aircraft in Alaska, and ICEALOT involved the deployment of the Woods Hole Research Vessel *Knorr* in the North Atlantic. Additionally, DOE led the Indirect and Semi-Direct Aerosol Campaign (ISDAC) as part of the IPY.

The CalNex campaign took place during the spring/summer of 2010, and was designed to build on existing California programs that address air quality and climate linkages. Under NASA's Earth Venture missions in the Earth Science System Pathfinder program, the Deriving Information on Surface Conditions from Column and Vertically Resolved Observations Relevant to Air Quality (DISCOVER-AQ) mission is conducting a series of field missions.

The overarching objective is to use targeted airborne and ground-based observations to improve the interpretation of satellite observations in diagnosing near-surface conditions relating to air quality. The first of the field studies was conducted over the greater metropolitan area of Baltimore, MD, with a complex multi-platform observing system, providing multiple perspectives on the factors that control air quality and influence the ability to monitor pollution events from space. Subsequent deployments were conducted in California's San Joaquin Valley in January 2013 and Houston, Texas, in September 2013. The DISCOVER-AQ mission will conduct a final deployment in Denver, Colorado, in summer 2014.

Field Campaign Websites

ARCTAS: http://www.espo.nasa.gov/arctas/
CalNex: http://www.esrl.noaa.gov/csd/calnex/
DISCOVER-AQ: http://discover-aq.larc.nasa.gov
ICARTT: http://www.esrl.noaa.gov/csd/ICARTT/index.shtml
INTEX-B: http://www.espo.nasa.gov/intex-b/index.html
INTEX-NA: http://cloud1.arc.nasa.gov/intex-na/
MILAGRO: http://www.eol.ucar.edu/projects/milagro/
NEAQS - ITCT 2004: http://www.esrl.noaa.gov/csd/2004/

POLARCAT: http://www.nilu.no/Portals/0/IMG/Forskning/NILU-Polaraaret-A4-web-NY.pdf
TRACE-P: http://www-air.larc.nasa.gov/missions/tracep/tracep.htm
TexAQS & TexAQS II: http://www.esrl.noaa.gov/csd/2006/

Satellite–Based Air Quality Observations

An extensive array of satellite-based systems (Appendix H) has been established by the United States and European Union countries to measure total atmospheric columns and limited vertical profiles of several key species. In the United States, these programs are led by the National Aeronautics and Space Administration (NASA) and the National Oceanic and Atmospheric Administration (NOAA). Non-government organizations have also played significant roles, such as the Harvard-Smithsonian Astrophysical Laboratory and the National Center for Atmospheric Research (NCAR). In Europe, the satellite measurements relevant to air quality are part of the large Global Monitoring for Environmental and Security (GMES) program, now renamed Copernicus. The satellite component is led by the European Space Agency (ESA) and the European Organization for the Exploitation of Meteorological Satellites (EUMETSAT). A number of other national programs, beyond the U.S. and European programs, provide relevant measurements (listed in Appendix H). NASA and ESA typically demonstrate new capabilities for Earth observations, while NOAA and EUMETSAT conduct long-term operational observations. Under U.S. programs, a suite of satellites including Terra, Aqua, Aura, CALIPSO (Cloud-Aerosol Lidar and Infrared Pathfinder Satellite Observation), as well as NOAA-17, NOAA-18, NOAA-19, and Suomi NPP (National Polar-orbiting Partnership), have been launched in the last two decades. Collectively, they measure columns and/or profiles of aerosol optical depth (AOD), O_3, H_2O, CO, CH_4, SO_2, NO_2, CFCs, other pollutants, and atmospheric parameters such as temperature, cloud properties, and water vapor. Most of these satellites have a near-polar low Earth orbit (LEO), passing twice per day over a given location. For many species, measurements are only possible during daylight, so only one measurement is made per day per instrument.

The Earth Observing System (EOS) Afternoon Constellation, or "A-Train," is a group of several of these satellites (Aqua, Aura, CALIPSO, CloudSat, and (previously) PARASOL (Polarization & Anisotropy of Reflectances for Atmospheric Sciences coupled with Observations from a Lidar) that fly in formation, crossing the equator a few minutes apart near 1:30 PM local time. The near-simultaneous observations from these satellites produce a rich picture of earth weather, climate, and atmospheric conditions. The OCO (Orbiting Carbon Observatory) mission, which suffered a launch vehicle failure in early 2009, was to join the A-Train to measure CO_2 with the precision required to map global distribution of CO_2 sources and sinks on regional scales. A U.S. replacement mission for OCO is scheduled for a July 2014 launch. In the meantime, Japan's Greenhouse gases Observing Satellite (GOSAT), launched in January, 2009, is globally monitoring CO_2, CH_4, and aerosols.

NOAA's National Environmental Satellite and Data Information Service (NESDIS) oversees operations of U.S. Geostationary and Polar-orbiting Operational Environmental Satellite programs (GOES and POES), providing imagery for weather forecasting and observations of light scattering relevant to aerosol characterizations. Under the GOES program, NOAA is scheduled to launch in 2016 the first of the GOES-R series of next generation geostationary weather satellites with the Advanced Baseline Imager (ABI). The ABI will provide aerosol optical depth measurements at a spatial resolution of 2 km every 5 minutes over the continental U.S. and Canada and, every 15 minutes, the entire disk of the northern and southern hemispheres. The Suomi National Polar-orbiting Partnership (NPP) satellite launched on October 28, 2011, with sensors such as OMPS (Ozone Mapping and Profiler Suite), VIIRS (Visible/Infrared Imaging Radiometer Suite), and CrIS (Cross-track Infrared Sounder), provides aerosol and trace gas information at much higher spatial resolutions than previously possible. For example, VIIRS aerosol optical depth and suspended matter (aerosol type) products are available at 750 m resolution. The joint NASA-NOAA Suomi NPP mission serves as a proving ground for the series of NOAA Joint Polar Satellite System (JPSS) operational satellites to be flown in the next two decades.

Beginning in 1995, ESA and EUMETSAT have flown a series of LEO satellites that typically provide measurements of these same air quality relevant species at approximately 9:30 AM local time (Ingmann et al., 2012). Europe is planning to continue these observations through the mid-2020's with the operational MetOp satellite series. Europe is also planning to continue and improve the data records available in the 1:30 PM orbit (currently provided from NASA Aura) by launching the Sentinel-5 precursor satellite (Veefkind at al., 2012) and Sentinel-5 missions in 2015 and 2022 respectively.

For the future, NASA and partner agencies are studying additional satellite platforms capable of measuring trace gases and aerosols to enhance the characterization of tropospheric air quality from space (NRC, 2007; Fishman et al., 2008; Fishman et al., 2012). The National Research Council (NRC) has recommended that NASA implement a number of "Decadal Survey Missions" over the next decade, in addition to implementing the JPSS and GOES programs.

These "Decadal Survey Missions" include the following:

(1)   The Geostationary Coastal and Air Pollution Events (GEO-CAPE) will partially focus on supporting air quality assessments and forecasts by measuring atmospheric columns with a frequency of one hour from a geostationary space platform.

(2)   The Active Sensing of CO_2 Emissions over Nights, Days, and Seasons (ASCENDS) mission will produce global atmospheric column CO_2 measurements without seasonal, latitudinal, or diurnal bias using simultaneous laser remote sensing.

(3)   The Aerosols, Clouds and Ecosystems (ACE) mission will consist of a lidar for characterizing aerosol height and properties, and a polarimeter for determining aerosol types.

(4)   The Global Atmospheric Composition Mission (GACM) will focus on ozone and related gases for intercontinental air quality and stratospheric ozone layer monitoring, from a LEO space platform.

Several nations (including the United States and countries in Europe and Asia) are currently planning to launch geostationary satellites capable of providing a common suite of air quality relevant measurements (O_3, NO_2, HCHO, aerosol, CO, SO_2, and other pollutant species) at hourly temporal resolution throughout daylight hours and at 5-10 km horizontal resolution (Committee on Earth Observation Satellites [CEOS], 2011). Geostationary Earth Orbit (GEO) satellites provide continuous observations over one part of the globe. A constellation of at least three GEO satellites can together provide hourly near-global observations of populated regions. Such observations will bring revolutionary new capability for satellite monitoring of emissions and receptor processes (Lahoz et al., 2012). Under the European GMES (Copernicus) program, ESA will launch the Sentinel-4 platform in 2019. The East Asia mission, Geo-KOMPSAT (Geostationary Korea Multi-Purpose Satellite) is led by the Korea Aerospace Research Institute (KARI) and scheduled to launch in 2018. GEO-CAPE is the NASA Decadal Survey mission under consideration in this category. In November 2012, NASA selected the Tropospheric Emissions: Monitoring of Pollution (TEMPO) proposal as the first investigation in the new Earth Venture-Instrument mission. TEMPO provides much, but not all, of the capability planned for GEO-CAPE atmospheric observations. The TEMPO instrument will be delivered in 2017 for an anticipated 2018 launch on a geostationary host satellite. TEMPO will be placed in an orbit location from which it can observe much of North America. TEMPO and the ESA and KARI missions will each provide hourly measurements of ozone, aerosols, and their precursors, such as NO_2, SO_2, and HCHO over their respective regions, together providing unprecedented highly space- and time-resolved observations of the Northern Hemisphere.

Satellite data complement surface networks and aircraft campaigns, and are essential tools for evaluating models and improving emissions inventories.
There has been inter-agency cooperation between the National Institute of Environmental Health Sciences (NIEHS), EPA, NASA, and NOAA in exploring the use of satellite observations to support epidemiologic studies. Satellite observations do not directly correspond to in situ measurements of pollutant concentrations. Thus, the use of satellite data for air quality forecasting, management, health effects studies, and climate change assessments is complex and involves integration of models and surface observations. While satellites offer global or near-global coverage of several important species, there are basic limitations in using a space platform to effectively probe the lower levels of the atmosphere where pollution exposures occur. Understanding these limitations is important for gauging how these systems can best complement ground-based networks and support air quality management assessments.

Attributes of Air Quality Satellite Data Products

Fundamental Limitations -- Most satellite air quality observations are based on spectroscopic techniques using reflected, scattered, or emitted solar radiation as a broad source of radiation. Although the science of measuring trace gases and aerosols from space is relatively mature, interference related to variable surface reflectivity, cloud attenuation, and overlapping spectra of other chemical species require significant data processing and treatment. Even with this sophisticated data retrieval, data products will contain spatial gaps for a given time period due to cloud interference and other issues, such as sun glint, etc. This is particularly true for instruments in a polar orbit, where the instrument may see an area only one time during the daytime. For example, aerosol events occurring at the same time as clouds are often screened as a result of cloud fractions being too high to produce an accurate aerosol optical depth (AOD) product for NASA's Moderate Resolution Imaging Spectroradiometers (MODIS) aboard the Aqua and Terra satellites.

Most satellite sensors sum over the entire column of air from satellite to ground, providing total column densities of trace gases or aerosols, whereas concentrations near the surface are used to define air quality. Some information on the vertical distribution of certain species can be obtained by using multiple observing angles for instruments in LEO, by limb sounding, active sensing, or other methods. For example, CALIOP aboard the CALIPSO satellite resolves aerosol vertical distributions every 30 meters. It is important to note that, for certain important trace gases (e.g., NO_2, SO_2, and HCHO) and aerosols, the majority of mass resides in the boundary layer of the lower troposphere, enabling associations linking column data to surface concentrations or emissions fields. In the eastern United States, reasonable correlations (Engel-Cox et al., 2004) have been developed between concentrations from ground level $PM_{2.5}$ stations and MODIS AOD using a fixed relationship. In the western United States, correlations are poor due to excessive surface light scattering from the relatively barren land surfaces. To better account for aerosols aloft, output from a chemical transport model has been applied to develop concentrations of $PM_{2.5}$ from MISR AOD (Liu et al., 2004).

In contrast to aerosols, most ozone resides in the stratosphere. Various techniques have been developed to extract the stratospheric signal to yield a tropospheric ozone residual (TOR), based on known homogeneities in the stratosphere and the use of chemical transport models and multiple measurements. Early approaches (Fishman, 1978), before and during the Total Ozone Mapping Spectrometer (TOMS) missions, combined limb (angled view to characterize the stratosphere) and nadir (downward view, characterizing the total column) techniques to derive tropospheric ozone residuals. The 2004 launch of NASA's Aura mission, with multiple ozone sensors, is starting to produce more refined tropospheric ozone maps. For example, direct derivation of tropospheric column ozone is possible from the Ozone Monitoring Instrument (OMI) on Aura (Liu et al., 2009). However, differentiating ozone in the boundary layer from that in the free troposphere continues to pose significant challenges.

This difficulty stems from strong molecular scattering of UV radiation in the boundary layer, and surface emission in the thermal IR range. Notably, the geostationary TEMPO instrument will make ozone measurements in both UV and visible (Chappuis-band) wavelengths to provide improved sensitivity to ozone in the boundary layer using multispectral retrievals.

Temporal Coverage -- The near polar orbiting tracks of most LEO satellites deliver at most twice daily snapshot measurements of trace gas species (approximately 12 hours apart). Measurements of many species can only be taken once during the single daytime overpass. Consequently, these instruments can only observe temporal patterns of pollutants or time-integrations of pollutant concentrations at daily or longer scales. Furthermore, instruments in LEO have only a short exposure to each Earth scene, limiting the signal-to-noise ratio. For many LEO products, observations for a given day are quite noisy, and weekly or monthly averages are more typically used. Geostationary (GEO) satellite platforms, such as the NOAA GOES systems (http://www.oso.noaa.gov/goes/index.htm), do provide near-continuous monitoring of physical parameters for weather tracking and forecasting purposes. The ability of a GEO instrument to observe an area for longer time periods potentially enables a sufficient signal-to-noise ratio to make short time period observations meaningful, on the order of one hour. TEMPO will provide the first-ever observations of tropospheric ozone and its precursors over North America from geostationary orbit.

Spatial Coverage -- Polar orbiting satellites typically provide horizontal spatial resolution between 10 and 100 km for atmospheric composition. Spatial resolution less than 10 km is possible with GEO and LEO platforms. Satellite observations of pollutants above the surface complement ground-based in-situ measurement networks – especially considering that a considerable fraction of pollutant mass resides well above the Earth's surface. As noted above, the sensitivity of satellites to pollutants at elevated heights can obscure measurements of the boundary layer, and, in general, satellite data products contain little or no information about the vertical distribution of pollutants.

Furthermore, one technique used to obtain vertical distribution information, the comparison of nadir and limb observations, is usable from GEO only if complementary limb observations are available from one or more polar orbiting satellites. The limitations of satellite data are further enumerated and elaborated (Vijayaraghavan et al., 2007) for the Global Ozone Monitoring Experiments (GOME) sensors for O_3, NO_2, and HCHO.

Measuring near-surface pollution is one of the most challenging problems for Earth observations from space. The NASA DISCOVER-AQ missions (2011-2014) are expected to help address this issue, along with some of the fundamental limitations discussed above. These missions are anticipated to help bridge the existing knowledge gap limiting the relevance of satellite observations to air quality. At the same time, they will provide insights into the potential benefits of higher time and space resolved measurements, as anticipated by GEO platforms.

Current Use of Satellite Data in Air Quality Management

In broad terms, satellite measurements serve as complements to other surface-based and aircraft measurement programs and air quality models. Satellite applications for air quality forecasting and assessments are covered extensively in the published literature (Martin, 2008; Fishman et al., 2008; Vijayaraghavan et al., 2007). The following summary describes how these data are most effectively incorporated in air quality assessments, albeit not capturing the full breadth of applications of satellite observations. Four general methods are applied in the use of satellite observations for air quality assessments:

Detecting Evidence of Long-Range Transport -- Satellite data support assessments of air quality on hemispheric and global scales, and assessments of long-range transport. These are projected to be of increasing importance to North American air quality management. Trans-oceanic air pollution transport can be observed with satellites, and direct observational evidence of this phenomenon has been clearly visible in satellite imagery (Figure 3).

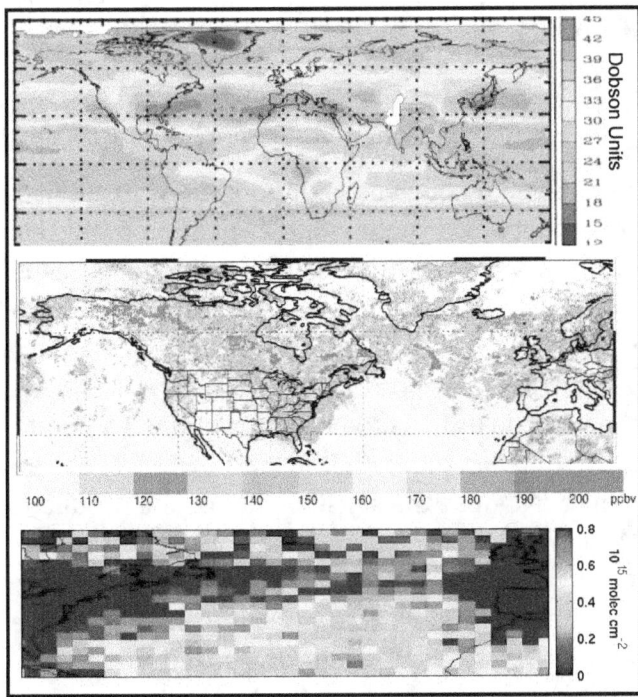

Figure 3. Panels capturing trans-Atlantic transport. Top: summer 1997 tropospheric ozone from GOME (Liu et al., 2006). Middle: CO column totals from MOPITT for July 2004 (Pfister et al., 2005). Bottom: Tropospheric NO_2 from SCIAMACHY for summer 2004 (Martin et al., 2006).

Characterizing Emissions and Air Quality Model Support -- Satellite observations play an important role in emissions characterization, particularly for source regions and sectors that have inadequate bottom-up inventories.

Applications include improving inventories from poorly-characterized, developing regions in Asia, and from "natural" sources such as lightning and soil NOx, biogenically emitted VOCs, wildfire particulate matter emissions, and agricultural based ammonia/NH_3.

The location and source strength of wildfire plumes detected from space serve as important inputs for annual emissions inventories (Martin et al., 2006; Soja et al., 2009) used in EPA air quality models, such as the Community Multiscale Air Quality Model (CMAQ), and processed as part of EPA's National Emissions Inventory. Satellite-based NO_2 (Wang et al., 2010) and SO_2 (Lu et al., 2010) data have illustrated the dramatic increases in Asian NOx and SOx emissions over the last decade. Increasing NOx and SOx emissions associated with gas and oil extraction from 2005 - 2010 in the Canadian oil sands have been identified by satellite NO_2 and SO_2 observations (McLinden et al., 2012). Biogenic VOC emission estimates have also been developed (Millet et al., 2008) using satellite measurements of formaldehyde, an oxidized product of directly-emitted isoprene. Advances in processing NH_3 signals from the Tropospheric Emission Spectrometer (TES) have led to improved spatial and temporal characterization of NH_3 surface patterns (Pinder et al., 2011), affording a potentially valuable tool to improve emissions estimates and evaluate models for sparsely measured air pollutants at the surface.

Air quality management depends on models for complex environmental characterizations that cannot be achieved through observations alone. Satellite-based enhancements to surface monitoring networks support the evaluation of these models by inter-comparison and improving emission inventories. Inverse modeling (the process of using a chemistry transport model (CTM) to estimate the emissions that reproduce the satellite observations) is frequently used in deriving "top-down" emissions that can improve and update emissions estimates from "bottom-up" inventories. Satellite observations of tropospheric ozone can be used as the basis for boundary condition inputs to regional air quality models. Satellite (OMI, GOME, and GOME-2) observations of NO_2 and HCHO can also be used to diagnose the sensitivity of ozone production to NOx or VOCs (Martin et al., 2004; Duncan et al., 2010).

Sustained long-term satellite observations support accountability analyses of the efficacy of environmental regulations. Due to a lack of surface-based true NO_2 measurements, satellite observations have been the most useful indicators of progress in the NOx State Implementation Plan (SIP) Call for Revision (Figure 4). Similarly, substantial declines in SO_2 emissions from coal power production facilities in the Eastern United States from 2005–2010, implemented through various cap and trade rules for major emission sources, are well correlated with satellite-derived, observed, SO_2 trends (Fioletov et al., 2011). A particular advantage of satellite observations is their ability to provide an abundance of observations with the same methodology across all locations on the planet. Consequently, global views emerge of pollutant trends capturing United States and European progress in emissions abatement, contrasted with emissions growth due to industrial expansion in Asia and elsewhere (Figure 5).

These success stories of infusing satellite observations into air quality assessments are notable as many of these "natural" and international emission source areas constitute a substantial fraction of atmospheric mass loadings that historically were generated without the benefit of an observation based evaluation component.

Serving as Surrogates to Filling Gaps in Surface Network -- Satellite observations are assisting the air quality community by providing data that cover broad spatial areas lacking ground-based monitors and, more importantly, a vertical (or column) complement to surface-based networks (Al-Saadi et al., 2005). Although 'breathing-zone' monitoring is essential, most pollutant mass resides outside the domain of surface stations. Pollutant levels aloft often correlate well with surface conditions during well-mixed afternoon conditions in stable pressure systems. This offers the potential for "gap filling" in the surface-based networks (Figure 6). However, the appeal of satellite observations to fill gaps in surface measurement must be tempered by the limitations of using space-based measurements to characterize near surface conditions.

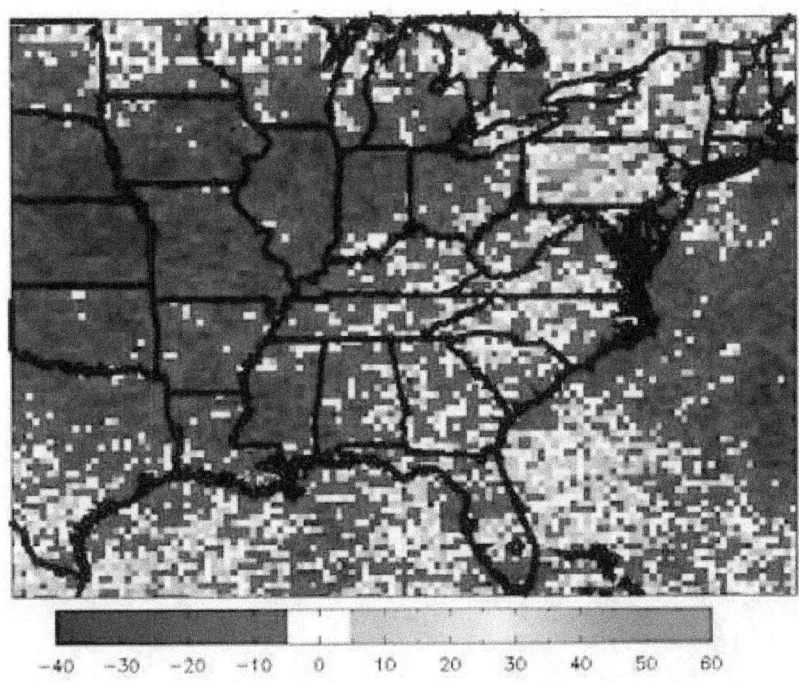

Figure 4. Percentage difference (July 2008 minus July 2005) in satellite-derived tropospheric NO_2 column amounts. Satellite data provide measurements that can be compared over large domains, suitable for trends analysis (Neil et al., 2009).

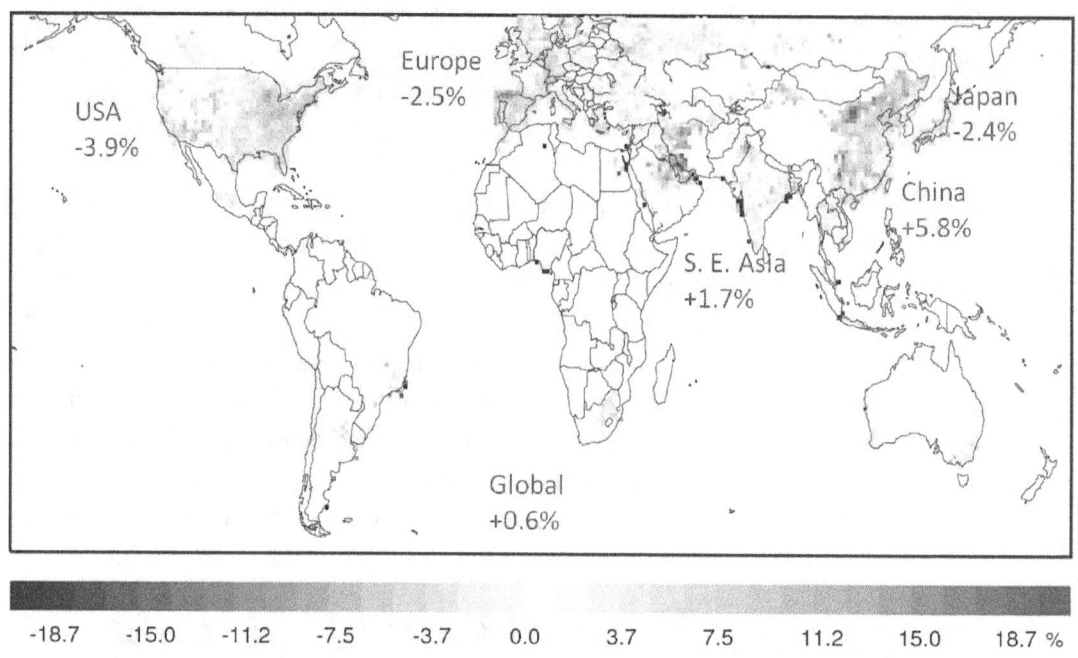

Figure 5. Percentage differences (2010 – 2005) in satellite-derived tropospheric NO2 column amounts based on OMI observations following the methodology of Lamsal et al., (2011).

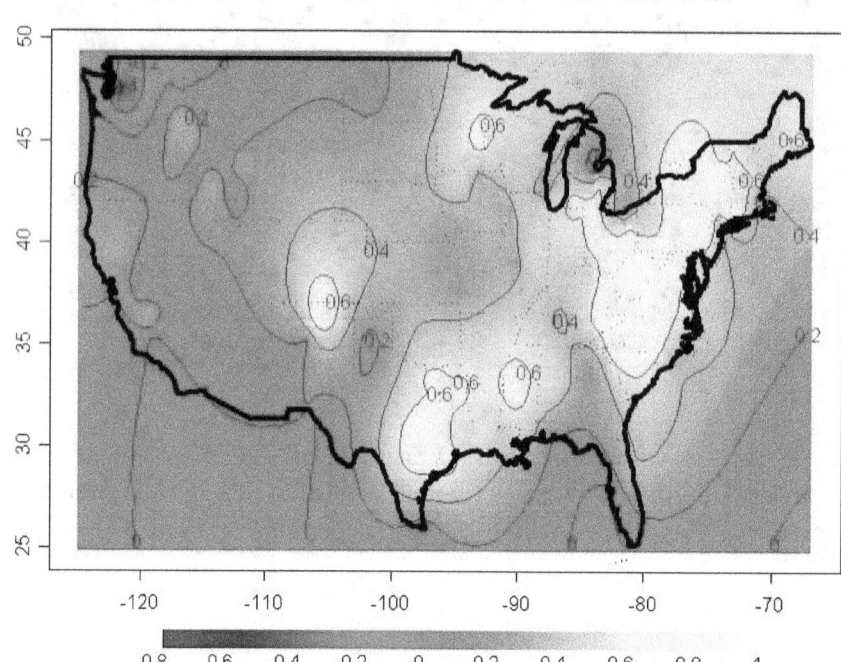

Figure 6. Correlation Coefficient between MODIS Aerosol Optical Depth (AOD) and hourly $PM_{2.5}$ surface sites from April - September, 2002 (Engel-Cox et al., 2004).

Providing Support During Episodes and Forecasting Air Quality -- Fire and dust events can produce atypically bad air quality in areas that do not usually experience poor air quality. Satellite data have played an important role in "exceptional event" analyses in determining attainment of the National Ambient Air Quality Standards. Satellite data can act as a surrogate for gaps in surface monitoring data, and the imagery can have an important public information role. Air quality forecast models rely on satellite data for verification (Al-Saadi et al., 2005; Kondragunta et al., 2008), offering the potential for assimilating aerosol and ozone gaseous precursor satellite data to constrain model predictions in field studies and next day air quality (Mathur, 2008; Pierce et al., 2009).

Observation Programs for Climate, Background Concentrations, Stratospheric Ozone, and Long-Range Pollutant Transport

NOAA and NASA are the lead Federal agencies for a variety of observation programs focused on climate change, background concentrations of trace gases in areas free of large local sources, stratospheric ozone, and pollutant transport. These data systems and networks include surface measurements, vertical profiling, and measurements of atmospheric columns (Appendix I). The Department of Energy (DOE) is also engaged in observation programs addressing climate change. Many of these observation programs rely on partnerships across U.S. Federal agencies and collaborations with international organizations, such as the World Meteorological Organization (WMO).

This section focuses on observation networks in the United States, which are largely the responsibility of NOAA, NASA, and DOE, with various levels of participation from partner agencies. The assortment of gases and aerosols that are important climate moderators and/or key air quality indicator and precursor species include: CO_2, N_2O, H_2O, CH_4, O_3, CO, aerosols, and halogenated compounds, including CFC replacements.

Greenhouse Gas (GHG) Observation Systems

NOAA, NASA, and DOE are lead Federal agencies for several programs addressing greenhouse gas trends, sources, sinks, and fluxes, many in partnership with each other and with international organizations. Although these programs are focused on carbon dioxide budgets, other important GHGs are included where feasible. In particular, methane (CH_4) acts as a strong climate forcing gas and influences global background levels of tropospheric ozone (West et al., 2007). The major GHG observation programs with sites in the United States include:

NOAA Global Cooperative Air Sampling Network -- This cooperative network includes over 100 remotely located surface stations worldwide, and a series of ship routes. Weekly samples from this network are used to determine global CO_2, N_2O, CH_4, and CFC concentration trends.

AmeriFlux Network -- DOE coordinates a multi-Federal agency group (with NOAA, USDA, NSF) overseeing the AmeriFlux network of ~90 active sites in the United States.

The network sites are largely micrometeorological towers ranging from a few to hundreds of meters in height. Each tower is instrumented with a fast CO_2 monitor and wind sensors, allowing calculation of the flux of CO_2 between the surface, vegetation, and the atmosphere. AmeriFlux is a component of the worldwide Fluxnet system of CO_2 flux networks, tracking storage of carbon in terrestrial systems (http://www.fluxnet.ornl.gov/fluxnet/index.cfm). The emerging NEON (National Ecological Observatory Network; http://www.neoninc.org/science/domains) is an NSF supported program that will provide 62 sites across the U.S., some of which are co-located with AMERIFLUX sites.

Vertical Profile, Atmospheric Column, and Satellite Observations -- The NOAA network of 8 tall towers (100 – 500 m) provides regionally representative, near-continuous, boundary layer measurements of CO_2 and related gases. As noted in Section 2, NASA's Orbiting Carbon Observatory (OCO) satellite mission was intended to be the Nation's primary remote sensing platform for CO_2, providing a continental and oceanic scale complement to ground based systems and aircraft programs. In light of OCO's 2009 launch failure, and delay of a replacement mission, climate monitoring relies for the present on Japan's Greenhouse Gases Observing Satellite (GOSAT). GOSAT was launched in January 2009, and measures CO_2 and CH_4 globally. Several United States and European satellite sensors (Aqua AIRS, NPP CrIS, and MetOp-1 IASI) also provide some profiling capabilities of greenhouse gases (O_3, CH_4, and CO_2) globally.

Monitoring of Background Air Quality and Long-Range Transport

Network of Remote (Sentinel) Surface Observation Stations -- Remote surface stations, located in areas relatively free from nearby sources, can characterize background pollutant levels, transport on regional and hemispheric scales, and boundary conditions for air quality models. NOAA maintains six baseline sites or surface "sentinel" stations designed to capture long-term trends and atmospheric background air pollutant concentrations (Mauna Loa, HI; Trinidad Head, CA; Barrow, AK; American Samoa; South Pole; and Greenland). These are part of a worldwide Global Atmospheric Watch (GAW) network of baseline sites coordinated by the WMO (Figure 7).

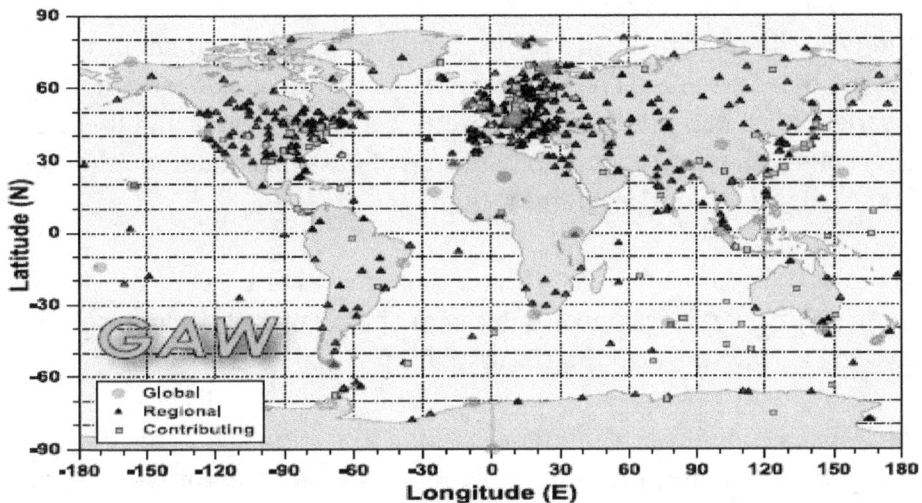

Figure 7. Network of surface-based remote observatories organized through the World Meteorological Organization's Global Atmospheric Watch (GAW).

NASA Fixed Site Observation Networks -- The AGAGE (Advanced Global Atmospheric Gases Experiment; http://agage.eas.gatech.edu/) and its predecessors (the Atmospheric Life Experiment, ALE, and the Global Atmospheric Gases Experiment, GAGE) monitor a variety of climate forcing gases, CFCs, and reactive trace gases at remote "sentinel" sites throughout the world.

Monitoring of Pollutants Aloft: Profiles and Total Columns

Vertical profiling and total atmospheric column measurements provide important complements to near surface observations. Observations aloft provide insight into background levels and transport phenomena, and are key metrics for model evaluation. It is difficult to rely on surface-based measurements to characterize these higher elevations because of complex near-surface deposition, removal, and micrometeorological processes. Programs to improve vertical profiles include a variety of aircraft, sondes (self-contained signal transmitters), remote sensing, tall towers, and special field programs.

These are largely managed by NOAA, NASA, NSF, and DOE. Proper siting and measurement techniques can produce observations that support assessments of climate change, stratospheric ozone, baseline concentrations, and long range and regional transport. These approaches include sampling throughout the atmospheric column (for total column and vertical profiles) and, particularly for fixed surface observations, measurements in locations that are relatively source free. Although climate and stratospheric ozone depletion assessments benefit from characterizing the full atmospheric column through the stratosphere (~35 km), systems designed to capture the entire atmospheric column often have insufficient resolution or precision in the boundary layer (~5 km) for surface-oriented air quality assessments.

NOAA Surface and Aircraft Based Air Quality Measurement Programs -- NOAA conducts a variety of routinely scheduled fixed-site and aircraft-based measurement programs, along with a series of intensive special field campaigns, to provide observations addressing a variety of climate, stratospheric ozone depletion, and planetary boundary layer air quality issues. These programs are a source of data on conditions aloft. Core elements of these measurement programs include:

- An ozone radiosonde network (8 sites, 4 in the United States) providing one day per week vertical ozone profiles with approximately 100m resolution from the surface through the stratosphere;

- The Dobson ozone spectrometer network (16 station cooperative network, 11 in the United States) providing near continuous daytime total atmospheric column ozone data;

- Routine aircraft flights that characterize the vertical distribution of air pollutant species (O_3, CO, CH_4, CO_2, N_2O, SF_6) for climate and air quality assessments;

- Tall tower sites (8) that are part of the larger interagency North American Carbon Program (NACP), designed to characterize carbon sources, sinks, and removal processes. These towers are currently located throughout the continental United States using television and cell phone towers (100 – 500 m tall). They provide near-continuous regionally representative boundary layer measurements of CO_2, CO, CH_4, and associated fluxes, various trace gases, and meteorological parameters (http://www.esrl.noaa.gov/gmd/ccgg/towers/index.html);
- Special intensive studies, often in collaboration with NASA, with aircraft focusing on regional U.S. air quality issues, typically conducted every two years (Section 2) and for satellite validation.

These programs, in combination with NOAA remote surface-based measurement observatories (http://www.esrl.noaa.gov/gmd/about/airquality.html), provide long term records of baseline air quality from the surface through the stratosphere. They represent a substantial component of the United States' contribution to international monitoring, much of which is organized through WMO's GAW program.

European-Based Aircraft Programs -- Two programs, MOZAIC (Measurement of OZone and water vapour by AIrbus in-service aircraft; operated since 1994) and CARIBIC (Civil Aircraft for the Regular Investigation of the Atmosphere Based on an Instrument Container; operated since 2004) measure air quality parameters from in-service, scheduled passenger aircraft based in Europe. These programs provide widely distributed, frequent, measurements in the upper troposphere, including over the Atlantic.

On takeoff and landing, they provide vertical profiles over cities, including cities in North America. These programs provide the most extensive, routinely-collected, vertically-distributed air quality data from throughout the troposphere.

MOZAIC: http://www.iagos.fr/web/rubrique3.html
CARIBIC: http://www.caribic-atmospheric.com/

Aircraft based observation programs are transitioning to the newly initiated IAGOS (In-service Aircraft for the Global Observing System) program, a partnership between European research institutions, universities, Airbus Industries, and commercial airlines around the world, including the United States. The purpose of IAGOS is to establish and operate a distributed infrastructure for long-term observations of atmospheric trace gases (O_3, CO, CO_2, CH_4, NOy, NOx, H_2O), particulate matter, and cloud droplet backscatter on a global scale. The initial fleet comprises 10 - 20 long-range in-service aircraft belonging to airlines based throughout the world. The data will be relevant for studies of air quality, long-range transport of pollution plumes, climate change, and the impacts of aviation on the composition of the atmosphere. The data will also be made available in near real-time for use by air quality forecast models, and in air quality modeling for environmental policy-making.

Satellite Air Quality Validation Programs -- NASA oversees the operation of several programs monitoring the lower atmosphere, designed to complement and evaluate satellite products described in Section 2. These programs generally have a broader hemispheric- or global-scale perspective, which often overlaps with regionally-focused initiatives.

Network for the Detection of Atmospheric Composition Change (NDACC) -- The NDACC is an international activity focused on obtaining high quality measurements of a broad range of atmospheric chemical species and parameters. This network includes more than 70 remote-sensing research stations. Originally focused on the stratosphere, with an emphasis on the ozone layer, the scope of the NDACC has expanded to cover both the stratosphere and troposphere.

A variety of working groups operate under NDACC, each focused on a particular measurement or technique, including Dobson/Brewer, FTIR spectrometers, lidar, microwave radiometers, satellite measurements, sondes, UV/Vis spectrometers, spectral UV, and water vapor. This network has been in operation since 1991 (http://www.ndsc.ncep.noaa.gov/).

Lidar Networks -- Lidar, analogous to radar, uses backscattered laser light to profile aerosols, gas-phase species, or other parameters, such as temperature, above a site. In addition to use during individual field studies, there are three fixed-site, long-term lidar monitoring networks in the United States.

The Micro Pulse Lidar Network (MPLNET) is coordinated by NASA, and operates from 14 stations (4 in the United States). MPLNET profiles aerosols, and most sensors are co-located with AERONET (see below). The NOAA CREST lidar network comprises four sensors that profile aerosols, and are operated by academic institutions in the eastern United States. Three of these sites can also profile water vapor. The international Network for the Detection of Atmospheric Composition Change (NDACC, described above) includes 17 lidars (3 in the United States). These networks are affiliated with a number of networks operating overseas in the WMO/GAW Aerosol Lidar Observation Network (GALION).

Selected Meteorological Observation Systems

Two categories of above-surface meteorological systems are included here because of their linkage to air quality assessments. First, solar radiation networks provide estimates of atmospheric aerosols and various trace gases, in addition to basic data for the radiation components of models. Second, systems that enable estimation of the height of the planetary boundary layer are important for near-surface air quality analyses and model applications.

Solar Radiation Networks -- Full spectrum and wavelength-specific solar radiation measurements provide data used to characterize energy budgets for meteorological models, climate change assessments, and atmospheric column aerosol light scattering. They also serve as direct indicators of UV radiation exposure, relevant to human and ecosystem health and agriculture. A variety of Federal agencies have participated in measurement programs, including NOAA, NASA, EPA, USDA, and the National Park Service.

The Aerosol Robotic Network (AERONET) is a NASA-organized, collaborative, global network of sun photometers providing ground-based aerosol optical depth (AOD) estimates used primarily to evaluate satellite aerosol measurements. NOAA's Surface Radiation Budget Network (SURFRAD) is part of the global Baseline Surface Radiation Network (BSRN). It is an important surface complement to satellites, and is used to characterize surface energy balances and support a variety of global scale climate models.

The Brewer UV spectrophotometer networks started in 1994 with EPA's UVNet program. UVNet included over 20 sites until funding ended in 2004. A subset of six sites supported by EPA and NOAA is operating as the NOAA-EPA Brewer Spectrophotometer UV and Ozone Network (NEUBrew). Brewer networks are designed to monitor UV radiation at the surface to understand effects on human and ecosystem health and agriculture. EPA has provided funding to study the relationship between changes in stratospheric ozone and UV at the surface. The Brewer instruments are capable of providing total column ozone and SO_2 estimates.

Observations for Evaluating PBL Heights -- Planetary boundary layer (PBL) height (or mixed layer height) is an important physical parameter in air quality models. PBL is a derived quantity based largely on vertical temperature profiles and refractive index structure parameters. The deployment of the NOAA Profiler Network (NPN: http://www.profiler.noaa.gov/npn/) over the last decade has added a near-continuous stream of wind vector data to complement the National Weather Service's (NWS) rawinsonde (radio tracked sonde) network, which provides twice daily soundings spread across nearly 100 locations throughout the United States. NPN consists of 35 unmanned Doppler radar sites profiling the troposphere, concentrated in the central United States and designed for forecasting violent weather. The PAMS program supports ~20 radar profilers that provide highly resolved wind profiles of the boundary layer. The boundary layer radar profilers, especially when complemented by temperature profiles generated by a Radio-Acoustic Sounding System (RASS), offer a source of relatively untapped data for model evaluation.

Cloud base height measurements from ceilometers are also reasonable PBL depth indicators for non-clear sky conditions. A spatially extensive network for broad application is available through the NOAA Automated Surface Observing System (ASOS). In addition, since 2004, over 400 commercial aircraft have been collecting meteorological variables (temperature, pressure, relative humidity, winds) as a part of the Tropospheric Airborne Meteorological Data Reporting (TAMDAR) system (http://www.airdat.com/technology/tamdar-sensor-network/). While TAMDAR is designed to provide near-real-time data for forecasting, the system provides valuable vertical profile temperature data (and other variables) during ascents and descents. These data can potentially be synthesized to fill temporal and spatial gaps in ground-based profilers.

The Meteorological Assimilation Data Ingest System (MADIS - http://madis.noaa.gov/) is an integrated system incorporating observations from a variety of surface-based, vertical profile, and satellite networks. MADIS ingests data files from NOAA and non-NOAA sources, decodes the data, and then encodes all of the observations into a common format with uniform observation units and time stamps. These surface and aloft meteorological data provide a finer density, higher frequency, observational database for use as inputs to air quality modeling systems that are designed to characterize air chemistry. Air chemistry and meteorological observations are used in combination for diagnosing air quality model behavior.

Maintaining and Advancing Observation Programs

Emerging challenges in air quality management will require pollutant monitoring programs to become both more comprehensive – that is, they will have to fill existing gaps -- and more integrated.

Measurement Gaps of Specific Species or Parameters

Nitrogen Species -- Nitrogen chemistry plays an important role in a variety of environmental problems, such as ozone, particulate matter, acidification, eutrophication, and visibility. Unfortunately, an adequate observation base does not exist to determine if ambient nitrogen responses are consistent with measured and predicted changes in NOx emissions resulting from recent regulations. The ability of the existing urban-oriented measurement network to detect ambient NOx changes associated with regional scale emission reductions from power stations is compromised by strong local NOx emissions. Also, NO_2 data from most network NOx monitors is affected by other oxidized nitrogen species. The NCore network will provide a modest advancement by measuring reactive nitrogen (NOy) in over 70 locations and, together with a more stringent NO_2 NAAQS (EPA, 2010), should spur greater coverage and deployment of instruments producing true NO_2 observations. True NO_2 is an important diagnostic species for atmospheric chemistry processes. These data are needed to validate satellite NO_2 observations and develop scaling of column data to boundary layer concentrations, facilitating the use of satellite data for locations without ground monitors.

Further measurements of oxidized nitrogen species, including peroxy acetyl nitrate (PAN) and nitric acid (HNO_3), would assist diagnosis of deposition and ozone production during atmospheric transport. Increased use of biofuels will potentially elevate PAN concentrations, and, along with observations of other carbonyl compounds, PAN will be an important indicator of the air quality impact of new fuels. Additionally, HNO_3 can be a key indicator species for understanding the NOx versus VOC limitation on ozone production in a given area.

Two reduced nitrogen species, gas-phase ammonia (NH_3) and particulate ammonium ion, are important components of nitrogen mass balance and for assessments of visibility, fine particles, and ecosystem deposition. There are few ambient NH_3 measurements, as most monitoring of this species occurs in strong source (agricultural) locations to estimate emissions flux. Also, ammonium ion is analyzed as part of the chemical speciation program, but NH_3 volatilization creates a negative bias in those values.

Routine measurements of nitrate radical (NO_3), the dominant nighttime oxidizer, at one or two representative locations would enable diagnosis of model predictions of overall nitrogen characterization.

Nitrous acid (HONO) is an important precursor of hydroxyl radicals (Stutz et al., 2004, Zhou et al., 2002), which are critical in daytime atmospheric chemistry. HONO also reacts heterogeneously with aerosols. Its sources and chemistry are not well understood, and are likely to be poorly characterized in air quality models. Among these needs, a reasonable priority would be to enhance measurements of true NO_2 and NH_3 in our national networks.

CO and SO_2 -- The atmospheric lifetime of carbon monoxide (CO) is one to three months, making it a useful tracer for evaluating emissions and physical process approximations in air quality models. Sulfur dioxide (SO_2) is the predominant precursor of sulfate, which is a major contributor to PM, acid precipitation, and regional haze. The available SO_2 and CO measurements are largely urban and often in proximity to major sources, limiting their representativeness for broader areas. In addition, most of the current instruments were designed to capture high concentrations for compliance purposes, and are not designed to measure the lower concentrations typical of rural areas. Column amounts of both CO and SO_2 available from sensors on current NASA research satellites are planned to be sustained on NOAA JPSS. In addition, the hourly CO measurements planned for GEO-CAPE will provide improved sensitivity to near-surface CO. The value of total column CO and SO_2 from satellites would be enhanced by more spatially rich surface observations.

Mercury -- Mercury has significant impacts on ecosystems and human health, but its chemistry in the atmosphere remains unclear. MercNet is a planning effort organized through NADP to standardize and network multi-media mercury measurements. This network will combine existing and new monitors to the extent possible. Speciated mercury measurements are important for model evaluation and tracking of emission reduction strategies, although the existing technology presents challenges in transitioning from research grade instruments to routine operations.

Volatile Organic Compounds -- Biogenically generated VOCs (isoprene, terpenes, sesquiterpenes) contribute significantly to the formation of ozone and secondarily formed $PM_{2.5}$. These compounds are not monitored by the urban-based PAMS or toxics networks, which are the primary sources of VOC data in the United States. The absence of VOC data in most moderately sized cities raises concerns regarding the overall representativeness of a network that is based primarily on the severity of ozone problems in the early 1990s. More troubling is the lack of rural VOC data, especially formaldehyde, a designated hazardous air pollutant (HAP) that is also used as a proxy for biogenic emissions and a useful diagnostic for model evaluations. Formaldehyde levels could also indicate alterations in atmospheric chemistry resulting from a future transition to alternative transportation fuels (e.g., alcohols or natural gas). The availability of more spatially rich surface observations would complement the value of total column formaldehyde measurements from satellites.

Organic PM Composition -- Planned programs to reduce emissions of inorganic precursors from mobile sources and power plants will increase the organic carbon fraction of the total aerosol budget. This effect is accentuated by large, uncontrollable organic emissions from biogenic and biomass burning sources. Chemical speciation networks provide an aggregated total organic carbon estimate, since it is not practical to resolve the full molecular spectrum of organic aerosols. Nevertheless, key molecular markers would assist source apportionment and distinguishing primary and secondary aerosol. Additional monitoring sites with representative mixes of aerosols and aerosol sources will be needed to supplement or replace current routine speciation analyses.

Aerosol Physical Properties -- Improved particle property measurements have been motivated by interest in near roadway and ultrafine particle exposures, particle nucleation processes, and tracking changes in aerosol size distributions associated with alternative transportation fuels (Wahlin et al., 2001). Recent advances in instrumentation produce relatively reliable and low cost estimates of particle number and surface area. These offer potential for application to routine network operations. This will necessitate additional permanent sites that capture long term changes in particle size characteristics. Particle size measurements could be incorporated into a more focused effort to characterize the range of particle and gaseous attributes associated with the near roadway environments.

Spatial Gaps

Integrated assessments necessarily deal with the behavior of pollutants over multiple spatial scales. This is because physicochemical processes occur on overlapping scales of time and distance. Matching actual pollutant exposure to individual humans requires monitoring at a finer spatial scale than provided by current networks. This is a key link in the source-to-outcome accountability chain. Primary emitted pollutants are subject to very dramatic gradients in the near-source region, including most of the 187 designated HAPs as well as a significant fraction of PM. These gradients often coincide with high population density. Characterization of regional- to urban-scale pollutant gradients provides insight on the relative contribution of regional and local sources to local pollutant levels.

Juxtaposed with the need for finer-scale monitoring is an emerging understanding of long range transport and a gradual rise in background pollutant levels. Rising background levels have resulted from increases in world-wide anthropogenic pollutant emissions. The relative significance of these background contributions to U.S. air quality is increasing, given the progress in North American pollution abatement relative to the increased atmospheric loading from expanding economies in Asia. As a result, monitoring pollutant flow across North American borders, as well as global tracking of "background" levels, has become increasingly relevant to North American multi-pollutant air quality management and accountability.

Spatial gaps in U.S. observation networks include:

Near Source - Fine Scale Characterization -- Ambient monitoring networks typically provide primary data to support a broad range of exposure, epidemiological, and risk assessment studies relating pollutant exposures to health outcomes. Epidemiological studies traditionally use air monitoring data from single, centrally-located urban stations as a surrogate for human exposure. However, urban environments in North America often have large and variable pollutant gradients raising uncertainties in outdoor and personal exposures. Neither of these issues is addressed effectively in current monitoring programs.

Internal Rural Coverage -- Three national networks form the backbone of rural air quality measurements: IMPROVE, CASTNET, and the NADP (Section 2). Although these networks were designed for specific objectives, they have also proven very useful for general air quality model evaluation and transport assessments. However, major spatial gaps exist in monitoring of surface-based ozone and key source indicator and precursor species (CO, SO_2, VOCs, speciated aerosol, NOx, and NOy) throughout the mid-section of the Nation (Figure 1 in Section 2). EPA's primary NAAQS, which are set to protect public health, have led to an urban focus in monitoring these species. Rising background pollutant levels (Cooper et al., 2010) have resulted from increases in world-wide anthropogenic pollutant emissions. This is particularly relevant to western mountainous regions, which are confounded by a mix of long distance pollutant transport, stratospheric ozone intrusion, increasing localized emissions from energy exploration and extraction operations, and population growth.

Sentinel Stations to Link Transport Regimes -- The addition of two or three remote stations on the east and west coasts of North America would support trans-oceanic transport assessments, global and regional air quality model evaluation, boundary conditions for models, and insight on background air quality trends. Sentinel sites need to be supported by a stable resource base, since their most significant benefit is often derived from analyzing long-term trends. Coincident measurements are needed of O_3 and aerosol components (nitrate, sulfate, organic and elemental carbon, trace metals), precursors of O_3 and aerosol (total reactive nitrogen, PAN, VOCs, and SO_2), and atmospheric tracers (such as CO, CO_2, and mercury). Because transported pollution is mostly aloft, sentinel stations are especially effective when they are located at altitude and/or include vertical profile measurements.

Vertical Profiles of Key Atmospheric Species -- Vertical profiling of boundary layer and free troposphere air chemistry in North America is limited to lidar networks, specialized field campaigns, and a small number of ozone sonde releases. The CALIOP instrument provides lidar profiles from space, producing several narrow "curtains" per day over the United States. More routine boundary layer profiling of meteorology and air chemistry would provide valuable support for model evaluation and emerging efforts to integrate models and observations.

Surface-based networks typically monitor the lower ten meters of the atmosphere, where most of the air we breathe is located. There are usually significant differences between this air and the PBL, which models attempt to characterize as a homogenous system. Coverage of these vertical transitions is difficult.

The rawinsonde network lacks adequate temporal resolution to adequately track the diurnal patterns of PBL heights, while NPN radar profiling does not provide sufficient vertical resolution for PBL characterization. Moreover, radar profilers have inadequate spatial coverage and lack consensus methodology to synthesize raw data into derived PBL heights conducive to model evaluation. Similar gaps were noted by a recent National Academies report on climate and weather observations (NRC, 2009b), which listed PBL height, air quality measurements above the PBL, and vertical profiles of humidity among the "highest priority observations needed to address current inadequacies."

Since satellite total column data do not simply correspond to surface conditions, routine vertical profiles of key species such as ozone, NO_2, CO, SO_2, and aerosols are needed to establish the relationship between surface-based point and satellite observations. This would increase the value of each system, and help satellite data fill gaps in sparsely monitored areas. Potential investments in vertical profiling programs to help leverage satellite data include:

- Expansion of NOAA's ozone sonde program to provide added spatial coverage in the continental United States, along with the addition of key trace gas measurements.

- A sustained U.S.-based aircraft campaign (national and international flights), similar to the European IAGOS (formerly MOZAIC and CARIBE) effort, to produce routine vertical profiles of key trace gases and aerosols.

- Deployment of fixed-site lidars (aerosol and/or ozone) at key locations throughout North America to provide continuous profiles of aerosol back-scattered light and ozone which can provide a direct link between ground-based, in-situ samplers and column densities from satellite instruments. NASA and NOAA are developing a small number of fixed-site and field-deployable ozone lidars through the Tropospheric Ozone Lidar Network (TOLNet) to assess the potential of such systems. Such a network could build on and complement the existing NDACC lidars and semi-routine aircraft-based measurements by NOAA.

Temporal Gaps

Temporal gaps in measurements include challenges in harmonizing continuous and gravimetric PM mass monitoring, and the lack of continuous or daily speciated particulate observations. As noted elsewhere, measurements from most satellites and sondes are only available once or twice per day, limiting their usefulness.

However, TEMPO in geostationary orbit will begin providing hourly satellite observations for several species when it launches later this decade.

The demand for higher temporal resolution for particulate matter observations has increased as a result of findings regarding human health response (Peters et al., 2001), and with our developing understanding of multi-scale atmospheric processes. With the exception of PM mass, particle properties are not monitored continuously on most networks. Consequently, surface based observations often miss parts of episodic events associated with fires and dust storms, in addition to limiting the number of pairings relating air quality to health outcome records.

While North American networks have deployed over 500 routinely operating continuous $PM_{2.5}$ mass samplers, harmonization of continuous and gravimetric (i.e., Federal reference) methods for PM mass remains a challenge. Measurement artifacts associated with the filter-based, gravimetric techniques creates significant ambiguity in the PM data, such as loss of mass of semi-volatile constituents. Harmonization could make continuous data more comparable with gravimetric data, allowing characterization of particle concentration distributions across large areas, but this could detract from efforts to produce "true" atmospheric aerosol measurements. Correlation techniques could avoid this problem. Eventually, harmonization of these measurements could address both temporal and spatial gaps in $PM_{2.5}$ monitoring.

Routine PM chemical speciation networks acquire 24-hour averaged samples, collected every third or sixth day. This sampling design is adequate for supporting the annual $PM_{2.5}$ standard and the U.S. regional haze program. However, the timing schedule limits the investigation of PM associations with adverse health effects, evaluation of emissions, development of air quality models, and application of source attribution techniques. Continuous PM speciation technology has been incorporated in the Supersites program, and light absorbing aethalometers (an indicator for elemental carbon) are included in the U.S. air toxics NATTS. Ten to twenty continuous sulfate and organic carbon analyzers are located in a mix of SEARCH and state or local agency platforms.

Satellite Observations

As surveyed in Section 2, satellites provide nominally global, daily monitoring of a number of species important for air quality and climate analyses. Recognizing the limitations noted previously, satellites can complement other monitoring systems. Both satellite and ambient observation systems become more valuable when they are integrated. Satellites observe parameters relevant to air quality where little or no routine in-situ monitoring occurs, such as over oceans and rural areas. Low Earth orbit missions provide near-global coverage, with limited temporal resolution and coverage.

Geostationary missions offer much better temporal coverage of a defined region and will begin acquiring observations over much of the Northern Hemisphere by the end of the decade. Although a tremendous advance will occur when TEMPO begins providing many of the measurements planned for GEO-CAPE in approximately 2018, a remaining challenge is to obtain the key companion observations, including CO and CH_4.

Current and future air quality satellite missions provide a stream of parameters directly relevant to air quality information for North America, and should strongly influence the design of our routine monitoring programs. These satellite data will improve near-term air quality characterizations and offer the potential to enhance air quality assessments. However, considerably greater value is realized from satellite observations when they are integrated with complementary ground-based point and vertical profile observations. This begins with validation efforts, when the algorithms used to produce column densities from raw satellite readings are refined and calibrated. Validation depends on independent measurements underneath the satellite. Several of the surface-based recommendations discussed above for trace gas measurements, such as formaldehyde, NO_2, CO, and SO_2, would be very helpful in validation. Intensive field studies have been useful to provide vertical information for satellite validation, but they have limited temporal and spatial coverage.

When validated, satellite data become useful for addressing spatial and/or temporal gaps in ambient monitoring through integration with existing monitoring networks. The integration of satellite information enhances both regional and global scale air quality characterizations, addressing important criteria pollutants such as O_3 and $PM_{2.5}$, and selected air toxics such as formaldehyde.

In addition to the technical challenges and limitations of using satellite data discussed above, it remains organizationally challenging for agencies, such as EPA, to effectively support planning and development of satellite missions.

Integration Opportunities

The assessment of any particular air quality issue, or related set of issues, is best served by the use of many types of observations and models. Likewise, these individual observations and data streams can serve multiple objectives, for disparate organizations and user communities. The integration of observations of different types, from different organizations, is both a major opportunity and a significant challenge.

Conceptually straightforward integration opportunities include:

- Enhancing the horizontal and vertical characterization of key species:
  - horizontally by combining urban- and rural-based networks (e.g., urban-based speciation networks with the rural-based IMPROVE program; SLAMs (urban) and CASTNET (rural) O_3 stations);

- vertically through the atmospheric column by blending surface measurements, vertically-resolved observations from ground-based and aircraft platforms, and satellite data;
- Combining precipitation and dry observation networks to develop deposition fields, as performed currently through the CASTNET and NADP programs;
- Collocating atmospheric deposition observations with soil and surface water measurement campaigns and select long-term ecological monitoring sites, such as NEON and the Long Term Ecological Research (LTER – www.lternet.edu) Network;
- Collocating a variety of different species measurements to yield multiple pollutant characterizations within a consistent spatial frame;
- Matching ambient measurement fields to human activity patterns to estimate exposures, and matching ambient measurements to emissions fields, via inverse modeling, to refine emission estimates;
- Using air quality models in combination with observations to address spatial and temporal gaps associated with limited observations.

Some of these examples are straightforward, like-to-like combinations of two networks with different but overlapping domains. Others, such as blending of satellite, surface, and aircraft data, or combinations of models with observations, are technically and scientifically challenging. Finally, organizational barriers exist for all of these recommendations, particularly for those that require moving monitors or modifying methods.

Observations and Models to Improve Environmental Characterization

Increasingly, models and observations are being used together, in a variety of ways, due to advances in computational efficiencies and in response to the complexities discussed in Section 1. Air quality models have typically been used in prognostic applications that address hypothetical questions regarding the effects of management programs and rules on future emissions and air quality changes – a function outside the scope of this observations report. More recently, air quality models have been used for forecasting (next day) air pollution, and providing more spatial texture beyond central site monitors to drive human exposure models. Observations alone lack adequate resolution (space, time, and composition) to support integrated assessments.

The integration of chemical observations and transport models is evolving, sharing common attributes with weather characterization and forecasting but less technically mature. Observation and model integration efforts range from using measurements to evaluate model performance, to four dimensional data assimilation (FDDA), as used in meteorological models.

Variations and intermediate levels of integration exist. Areas of observation-model linkages include:

- Model results to guide monitoring site design for placement in areas of expected high concentrations, steep concentration gradients, and important transport corridors;
- Observations supplying direct inputs for initial and/or boundary conditions in models;
- Observations to indirectly improve model inputs through inverse modeling of emissions;
- Observations to evaluate model performance, diagnose model behavior, and constrain model adjustments;
- Observations combined or "fused" with model estimates to add spatial, temporal, and compositional texture to air quality gradients; and,
- Dynamic assimilation of observations to nudge model estimates, analogous to FDDA in meteorological systems.

The linkages between observations and models are emphasized here as a means to influence a shift in monitoring design to explicitly recognize these relationships.

Information Technology to Facilitate Data Access, Integration, and Use

Integrated air quality management requires technology to facilitate discovery, access, handling, archiving, and harmonization of numerous disparate information sources. Accessing and handling observations from single networks or databases remain a challenge, despite large investments. Some applications and tools to access and integrate multiple data systems have eased the integration of disparate data from multiple programs, but by and large differing formats, standards, and gaps in metadata significantly hamper integration of different types of data and models. This prevents analysts from realizing the full value of air quality data.

The EPA system for accessing air quality observations was designed primarily as a repository for data, and covers only a part of U.S. observational archives. Several other organizations have recently built publicly accessible, user-friendly, air quality data reduction, integration, analysis, and visualization systems. These include VIEWS, the Visualization Information Exchange Web System developed by the Regional Planning Organizations (RPOs; http://views.cira.colostate.edu/web/) in support of visibility assessments, the Health Effects Institute's air quality database (Section 2), and ADAM (Airborne Data for Assessing Models; http://www-adam.larc.nasa.gov/main.htm). NARSTO (http://www.narsto.org/) also has constructed an accessible database for intensive field campaigns of historical interest.

GEOSS, the Global Earth Observation System of Systems (Appendix A), is a current effort to build a framework to enable national governments to make Earth science data more accessible and usable for decision support.

GEOSS is designed to make data easier to find and access, as well as to support a service-oriented, interoperable, systems approach. This is in contrast to the end-to-end systems typically built to process, handle, and visualize air quality and satellite data. The GEOSS approach is designed to produce more cost-effective, nimble, and usable tools to allow analysts to integrate different types of monitoring data, models, and emissions inventories, etc. This approach has been demonstrated and piloted by several Federally supported projects, including:

- DataFed (http://datafedwiki.wustl.edu/index.php/DataFed_Wiki), which mediates between autonomous, distributed, air quality data providers and users. This facilitates access to and flow of atmospheric data from provider to users, supporting the development of user-driven data processing value chains and improving inputs to comprehensive integrated environmental assessments.

- GEOSS Architecture Implementation Pilot (AIP) Air Quality Workgroup, which developed the GEOSS infrastructure for air quality data and built "Air Quality Community Infrastructure" to serve as an interface between air quality analysts and GEOSS.
  https://sites.google.com/site/geosspilot2/air_quality-and-health-working-group

- Cyberinfrastructure for Air Quality Management (CyAir), which contributes to the planning, development, maintenance, and coordination of systems to help the air quality community better utilize air quality information. The cyberinfrastructure is envisioned as a service-oriented, open-source, web-based network of air quality and pollutant emissions data providers and repositories, supported by existing and new data analysis tools for use by the air quality management and research communities.
  http://cyair.net

These emerging integrated systems will help address technology needs for comprehensive assessments, but will require substantial, sustained investment and engagement from supporting and user communities.

Barriers to Progress

Any approach to addressing the emerging air quality and assessment issues must recognize the resource, technological, and institutional constraints that impede the progress of air quality monitoring programs.

Sustaining Infrastructure

As documented in many fields of endeavor, it is challenging for organizations to maintain infrastructure. Monitoring systems are no different. Users are often in different organizations than providers, and take the data for granted. Indeed, the provision of seamless, automated access to data lets users work with minimal awareness of who produced the data.

Many measurement networks struggle with outdated technology, old equipment, and aging workforces. Downstream assessments are more visible than the monitoring systems that support them, the latter being sustained by a "trickling down" of resources.

Organizational Priorities

Organizations often lack the resource flexibility to support medium or low priority measurements. For example, EPA relies on Federal Reference Methods (FRM) and Federal Equivalent Methods (FEM) to assess compliance with air quality standards. Under constrained budgets, new and improved measurements of high scientific value are generally difficult to fund. A recent example is the continued acceptance of existing NOx instruments with known biases, despite development of a new NO_2 standard.

Transitioning Research and Technology Development to Operations

Measurement programs supported by research organizations are particularly vulnerable to loss of funding, compromising long-term records and other applications. In the case of satellites, "research" sensors/platforms with finite lifetimes are typically not replaced. Although analysis of long-term air quality patterns is a research interest, research organizations typically focus on methods development and physicochemical process characterization. The expectation is that routine measurement programs will transition to operational organizations. For example, NASA satellite missions have defined operational time spans, yet the transition to longer term operational status through partner agencies is generally not planned in advance. Successful transitions have included the LANDSAT mission partnership between USGS and NASA, as well as EPA's management of CASTNET, which was transitioned from EPA's research office to EPA's air office in the late 1990s.

The original NCore monitoring strategy for proposed Level 1 sites had been to form partnerships between universities and state and local agencies to test emerging instrumentation, and jointly share in the transition of research grade equipment to operations. However, Level 1 sites have not been deployed, even though more than 70 Level 2 multiple pollutant measurement sites relying on routine instruments have been deployed. As a result, there has been inadequate incorporation of continuously operated speciated particulate matter, mercury, and inorganic nitrogen species (reduced and oxidized forms) measurements.

Challenges of Long-Term Support for Future Satellite Missions

A particular research-to-operations challenge is the difficulty that recipient agencies face in supporting the development and funding of future satellite missions. Satellite instruments are planned, developed, and funded years before the platform is launched, due partly to the high costs associated with satellite missions. This time frame often extends beyond the planning time horizon of a regulatory agency.

EPA does not fund satellite missions, but it would be useful for it and other recipient agencies to have a mechanism to identify how specific instruments/missions will jointly help monitor and manage ambient air quality. Although it is difficult for a recipient agency to commit to use data many years in the future, such commitments could influence mission funding and instrument design decisions. Conversely, satellite instruments have proven essential for air quality analysis and management, and the provision of data to address emerging air quality assessment challenges should remain high in mission agency planning priorities.

Market Incentives

Beyond the need for FRM/FEM instruments, there are few market incentives for instrumentation firms to pursue the engineering and development steps necessary to produce operational grade methods. This financial barrier is linked to the above noted issues regarding agency priorities, transition from research to operations, and communication impediments between regulatory agencies and instrument developers over anticipated future needs.

Observation technology is typically developed by individual research groups for specific applications associated with a laboratory or field campaign objective. This technology can then be passed on to other users. For example, NASA develops satellite observation platforms in space and on aircraft typically for single-use (or short-term), promising technologies. These are then transferred to NOAA, and the satellite sensors made operational by NESDIS. There is no similar development path for technologies to inform surface air chemistry monitoring for use by EPA or state and local air quality managers.

Conclusions

The United States has a robust and invaluable network of air quality observation systems, and recent improvements in technology are providing unprecedented opportunities to enhance current capabilities. However, there also exist substantial opportunities for improvement in the U.S. air quality observation system as currently implemented.

Establish Standing Multi-Agency Observations Working Group

As a first step to taking advantage of these opportunities, the NSTC should consider chartering an interagency working group on air quality observations under the AQRS of the CENRS. This group would maintain close coordination with national Civil Earth Observations planning and the U.S. Group on Earth Observations (USGEO) activities, including consideration of existing partnership models (e.g., NADP, IMPROVE). The objectives of this working group could include:

- Provide a forum to facilitate cooperation and collaboration among the Federal agencies with air quality observation programs. Air quality measurements are important to so many users that a broader view of the health, relevancy, and evolution of observation programs should complement the existing single-organization focus on discrete network elements.
- Provide an interface between the various user communities (e.g., air quality managers, health scientists, air quality forecasters, etc.) and those involved in making air quality observations to ensure the benefits are maximized for both communities.

- Extend the analysis presented in this report and develop specific recommendations for improvements to the Nation's air quality observing system and track progress towards the goals established. Specifically, the Working Group on Air Quality Observations would:
    - assess the adequacy of current networks and measurement technologies, including maintenance shortfalls and modernization needs
    - identify important measurement gaps
    - identify important information gaps and opportunities for advancing technology and sharing and utilization of observation programs.
- Coordinate the development of multi-agency initiatives to address deficiencies that have been identified and enhance and extend air quality observations in the U.S.

Address Current Observation Gaps

Numerous important measurements that are missing or in short supply were described in Section 3. This analysis will need to be revisited as monitoring systems and our understanding of the atmosphere evolve, and it will be appropriate for the working group to add their perspective to the analysis presented there.

While requests for added observations have been raised periodically, this renewed effort is intended to (a) increase the overall value-to-cost ratio incurred collectively through a system of measurement programs and (b) improve the comprehensive effectiveness of measurement programs where past requests have focused on specific topics without recognition of the broader opportunities for leverage and cooperation. Suggested steps include:

1. initiate monitoring of reactive gas and particulate nitrogen compounds, which are precursors of ozone and particulate matter, contributors to acid deposition, and nutrients in ecosystems,
2. collocate instrumentation at core monitoring sites to facilitate inter-comparison with satellite observations,
3. target monitoring in rural/remote areas to measure regional backgrounds and contributions from long-range transport of pollutants,
4. establish more robust air toxics monitoring near major industrial facilities to help investigate whether air toxics emissions are associated with human health effects in nearby communities,
5. target intensive field studies designed to elucidate critical processes that determine atmospheric concentrations of ozone and particulate matter and other air pollutants, and
6. establish routine monitoring of vertically resolved observations of ozone, fine particulate matter (including its composition), and their precursors, to evaluate and improve air quality modeling.

References

Al-Saadi, J., J. Szykman, R.B. Pierce, C. Kittaka, D. Neil, D.A. Chu, L. Remer, L. Gumley, E. Prins, L. Weinstock, C. MacDonald, R. Wayland, F. Dimmick, and J. Fishman, 2005: Improving national air quality forecasts with satellite aerosol observations. Bull. Am. Met. Soc., 86, 1249-1261.

Committee on Earth Observation Satellites, 2011: A geostationary satellite constellation for observing global air quality: An international path forward. CEOS Atmospheric Composition Constellation, Draft ACC White Paper v4, 41 pp. (available at http://www.ceos.org/index.php?option=com_content&view=article&id=64:2008-07-25-14-45-59&catid=54:acc-documents&Itemid=95)

Cooper, O.R., D.D. Parrish, A. Stohl, M. Trainer, P. Nedelec, V. Thouret, J.P. Cammas, S.J. Oltmans, B.J. Johnson, D. Tarasick, T. Leblanc, I.S. McDermid, D. Jaffe, R. Gao, J. Stith, T. Ryerson, K. Aikin, T. Campos, A. Weinheimer, and M.A. Avery, 2010: Increasing springtime ozone mixing ratios in the free troposphere over western North America. Nature, 463, 344-348.

Duncan, B., Y. Yoshida, J. Olson, S. Sillman, R. Martin, L. Lamsal, Y. Hu, K. Pickering, C. Retscher, D. Allen, and J. Crawford, 2010: Application of OMI observations to a space-based indicator of NOx and VOC controls on surface ozone formation. Atmos. Environ., 44, 2213-2223, doi:10.1016/j.atmosenv.2010.03.010.

Environmental Protection Agency, 1997: National Ambient Air Quality Standards for Particulate Matter. CFR, Part 50, Title 40.

Environmental Protection Agency, 2006: Revisions to Ambient Air Monitoring Regulations. CFR Parts 53 and 58, 71 FR 61236, October 17, 2006.

Environmental Protection Agency, 2008: Ambient Air Monitoring Strategy for State, Local, and Tribal Air Agencies. Office of Air Quality Planning and Standards, Research Triangle Park, NC. (available at http://www.epa.gov/ttn/amtic/monstratdoc.html)

Environmental Protection Agency, 2010: Primary National Ambient Air Quality Standards for Nitrogen Dioxide. 40 CFR Parts 50 and 58, 71 FRL 9107-9, February 9, 2010. (available at http://www.epa.gov/ttn/naaqs/standards/nox/fr/20100209.pdf)

Engel-Cox, J.A., C.H. Holloman, B.W. Coutant, R.M. Hoff, 2004: Qualitative and quantitative evaluation of MODIS satellite sensor data for regional and urban scale air quality. Atmos. Env., 38, 2495-2509.

Fehsenfeld, M. Trainer, D.D. Parrish, A. Volz-Thomas, and S. Penkett, 1996: North Atlantic Regional Experiment 1993 summer intensive: Foreword. J. Geophys. Res., 101, 28,869-28,875.

Fehsenfeld, F. C., G. Ancellet, T.S. Bates, A.H. Goldstein, R.M. Hardesty, R. Honrath, K.S. Law, A.C. Lewis, R. Leaitch, S. McKeen, J. Meagher, D.D. Parrish, A.A.P. Pszenny, P.B. Russell, H. Schlager, J. Seinfeld, R. Talbot, R. Zbinden, 2006: International Consortium for Atmospheric Research on Transport and Transformation (ICARTT): North America to Europe – Overview of the 2004 summer field study. J. Geophys. Res., 111, D23S01, doi:10.1029/2006JD007829.

Fioletov, V.E., C.A. McLinden, N. Krotkov, M.D. Moran, and K. Yang, 2011: Estimation of SO_2 emissions using OMI retrievals. Geophysical Research Letters, Vol. 38, L21811, doi:10.1029/2011GL049402.

Fishman, J., and P. J. Crutzen, 1978: The Origin of Ozone in the Troposphere. Nature, 274, 855-858.

Fishman, J., et al., 2008: Remote Sensing of Tropospheric Pollution from Space. Bull. Am. Met. Soc., 89(6), 805-821.

Fishman et al., 2012: The United States' Next Generation of Atmospheric Composition and Coastal Ecosystem Measurements: NASA's Geostationary Coastal and Air Pollution Events (GEO-CAPE) Mission. Bull. Am. Met. Soc. doi: 10.1175/BAMS-D-11-00201.1 http://journals.ametsoc.org/doi/pdf/10.1175/BAMS-D-11-00201.1

Geller, M.D., and P.A. Solomon, 2006: Special Issue of Aerosol Science and Technology for Particulate Matter Supersites Program and Related Studies. Aerosol Sci. and Tech., 40, 10,735-736.

Keating, T. and A. Zuber, 2007: Hemispheric Transport of Air Pollution 2007, Interim Report prepared by the Task Force on Hemispheric Air Pollution. United Nations Publication ISSN 1014-4625.

Kondragunta, S., P. Lee, J. McQueen, C. Kittaka, A.I. Prados, P. Ciren, I. Laszlo, R.B. Pierce, R. Hoff and J. Szyman, 2008: Air Quality Forecast Verification Using Satellite Data. AMS, DOI: 10.1175/2007JAMC1392.1

Ingmann, P., B. Veihelmann, J. Langen, D. Lamarre, H. Stark, G. Bazalgette Courrèges-Lacoste, 2012: Requirements for the GMES Atmosphere Service and ESA's implementation concept: Sentinels-4/-5 and -5p. Remote Sensing of Environment, Volume 120, 15 May 2012, Pages 58-69, ISSN 0034-4257, 10.1016/j.rse.2012.01.023. (http://www.sciencedirect.com/science/article/pii/S0034425712000673)

Lahoz, W.A., V.-H. Peuch, J. Orphal, J.-L. Attié, K. Chance, X. Liu, D. Edwards, H. Elbern, J.-M. Flaud, M. Claeyma n, and L. El Amraoui, 2012: Monitoring Air Quality From Space: The Case for the Geostationary Platform. Bull. Am. Met. Soc, DOI:10.1175/BAMS-D-11-00045.1

Lamsal, L.N., R.V. Martin, A. Padmanabhan, A. van Donkelaar, Q. Zhang, C.E. Sirois, K. Chance, T.P. Kurosu, and M.J. Newchurch, 2011: Application of satellite observations for timely updates to global anthropogenic NOx emissions inventories. Geophysical Research Letters, Vol. 38, L05810, doi:10.1029/2010GL046476.

Liu, Y.; Park, R. J.; Jacob, D. J.; Li, Q. B.; Kilaru, V.; Sarnat, J. A., 2004: Mapping annual mean ground-level PM2.5 concentrations using Multiangle Imaging Spectroradiometer aerosol optical thickness over the contiguous United States. Journal of Geophysical Research-Atmospheres 2004, 109, (D22).

Liu, X., K. Chance, C.E. Sioris, T.P. Kurosu, R.J.D. Spurr, R.V. Martin, T. Fu, J.A. Logan, D.J. Jacob, P.I. Palmer, M.J. Newchurch, I.A. Megretskaia, R.B. Chatfield, 2006: First directly retrieved global distribution of tropospheric column ozone from GOME: Comparison with the GEOS-CHEM model. J. Geophys. Res., 111, D02308, doi:10.1029/2005JD006564.

Liu, X., P. K. Bhartia, K. Chance, R. J. D. Spurr, and T. P. Kurosu, 2009: Ozone profile retrievals from the Ozone Monitoring Instrument. Atmos. Chem. Phys. Discuss., 9, 22693-22738.

Lu, Z., D.G. Streets, Q. Zhang, S. Wang, G.R. Carmichael, Y.F. Cheng, C. Wei, M. Chin, T. Diehl, and Q. Tan, 2010: Sulfur dioxide emissions in China and sulfur trends in East Asia since 2000. Atmos. Chem. Phys., 10, 6311-6331.

Martin, R.V, A. Fiore, and A. van Donkelaar, 2004: Space-based diagnosis of surface ozone sensitivity to anthropogenic emissions. Geophys. Res. Lett., 31,L06120, doi:10.1029/2004GL019416.

Martin, R.V., C.E. Sioris, K. Chance, T.B. Ryerson, T.H. Bertram, P.J. Wooldridge, R.C. Cohen, J.A. Neuman, A. Swanson, F.M. Flocke, 2006: Evaluation of space-based constraints on global nitrogen oxide emissions with regional aircraft measurements over and downwind of eastern North America. J. Geophys. Res., 111, D15308, doi:10.1029/2005JD006680.

Martin, R. V., 2008: Satellite remote sensing of surface air quality. Atmos. Environ., 42, 7823-7843.

Mathur, R., 2008: Estimating the impact of the 2004 Alaskan forest fires on episodic particulate matter pollution over the eastern United States through assimilation of satellite-derived aerosol optical depths in a regional air quality model. J. Geophys. Res., doi:10.1029/2007JD009767.

McLinden, C.A., V. Fioletov, K.F. Boersma, N. Krotkov, C.E. Sioris, J.P. Veefkend, and K. Yang, 2012: Air quality over the Canadian oil sands: A first assessment using satellite observations. Geophysical Research Letters, Vol. 39, L04804, doi:10.1029/2011GL050273.

Millet, D.B., D.J. Jacob, K.F. Boersma, T. Fu, T.P. Kurosu, K. Chance, C L. Heald, and A. Guenther, 2008: Spatial distribution of isoprene emissions from North America derived from formaldehyde column measurements by the OMI satellite sensor. J. Geophys. Res., 113, D02307, doi:10.1029/2007JD008950.

National Research Council (NRC), 1991: Rethinking the Ozone Problem in Urban and Regional Air Pollution. National Academy of Sciences Press, Washington, DC.

National Research Council (NRC), 2004: Air Quality Management in the United States. The National Academies Press, Washington, DC.

National Research Council (NRC), 2007: Earth Science and Applications from Space: National Imperatives for the Next Decade and Beyond. The National Academies Press, Washington, DC.

National Research Council (NRC), 2009a: Global Sources of Local Pollution: An Assessment of Long-Range Transport of Key Air Pollutants to and from the United States. The National Academies Press, Washington, DC.

National Research Council (NRC), 2009b: Observing Weather and Climate from the Ground Up: A Nationwide Network of Networks. The National Academies Press, Washington, DC.

Neil, D.O., S. Kondragunta, G. Osterman, K. Pickering, R.W. Pinder, A. Prados, and J. Szykman, 2009: Satellite Observations for Detecting and Tracking Changes in Atmospheric Composition. EM, October 2009, 13-15.

Pandis, S., P.A. Solomon, and R. Scheffe, 2005: Preface to special section on Particulate Matter Supersites. J. Geophys. Res., doi :10.1029/2005JD005983.

Penkett, S.A., A. Volz-Thomas, D.D. Parrish, R.E. Honrath, and F.C. Fehsenfeld, 1998: North Atlantic Regional Experiment (NARE II): Preface. J. Geophys. Res., 103, 13,353-13,355.

Peters, A., D.W. Dockery, J.E. Muller, and M.A. Middleton, 2001: Increased particulate air pollution and the triggering of myocardial infarction. Circulation, 103, 2810-2815.

Pfister, G., P. G. Hess, L. K. Emmons, J.-F. Lamarque, C. Wiedinmyer, D. P. Edwards, G. Pétron, J. C. Gille, and G. W. Sachse, 2005: Quantifying CO emissions from the 2004 Alaskan wildfires using MOPITT CO data. Geophys. Res. Lett., 32, L11809, doi:10.1029/2005GL022995.

Pierce, R.B., J.Al-Saadi, C. Kittaka, T. Schaack, A. Lenzen, K. Bowman, J. Szykman, A. Soja, T. Ryerson, A. M. Thompson, P. Bhartia, and G. A. Morris, 2009: Impacts of background ozone production on Houston and Dallas, Texas air quality during the Second Texas Air Quality Study field mission. Journal of Geophysical Research - Atmospheres 114.D00F09 (2009): doi:10.1029/2008JD011337.

Pinder, R.W., J.T. Walker, J.O. Bash, K.E. Cady-Pereira, D.K. Henze, M. Luo, G.B. Osterman, and M.W. Shephard, 2011: Quantifying spatial and seasonal variability in atmospheric ammonia with in situ and space-based observations. Geophysical Research Letters, Vol. 38, L04802, doi:10.1029/2010GL046146.

Pope, C.A., M. Ezzati, M., and D.W. Dockery, 2009: Fine-particulate air pollution and life expectancy in the United States. N Engl J Med, 360, 376-386.

Scheffe, R. D., P.A. Solomon, R. Husar, T. Hanley, M. Schmidt, M. Koerber, M. Gilroy, J. Hemby, N. Watkins, M. Papp, J. Rice, J. Tikvart, R. Valentinetti, 2009: The National Ambient Air Monitoring Strategy: Rethinking the Role of National Networks. J. Air & Waste Manage. Assoc., 59, 1-12.

Soja, A.J., J. Al-Saadi, L. Giglio, D. Randall, C. Kittaka, G. Pouliot, J.J. Kordzi, S. Raffuse, T.G. Pace, T.E. Pierce, T. Moore, B. Roy, R.B. Pierce, and J.J. Szykman, 2009: Assessing satellite-based fire data for use in the National Emissions Inventory. Journal of Allied Remote Sensing, Vol. 3, 031504.

Solomon, P., E. Cowling, G. Hidy, C. Furiness, 2000: Comparison of scientific findings from major ozone field studies in North America and Europe. Atmospheric Environment, Vol: 34, Issue: 12-14, Pages: 1885-1920.

Solomon, P.A., P.K. Hopke, J. Froines, and R. Scheffe, 2008: Key Scientific and Policy- and Health-Relevant Findings from the U.S. EPA's Particulate Matter Supersites Program and Related Studies: An Integration and Synthesis of Results. J. Air & Waste Manage. Assoc., 58, S-1 – S-92.

Stutz, J., B. Alicke, R. Ackermann, A. Geyer, S.H. Wang, A.B. White, E.J. Williams, C.W. Spicer, and J.D. Fast, 2004: Relative humidity dependence of HONO chemistry in urban areas. J. Geophys. Res., 109, doi:10.1029/2003JD004135.

Veefkind, J.P,, I. Aben, K. McMullan, H. Förster, J. de Vries, G. Otter, J. Claas, H.J. Eskes, J.F. de Haan, Q. Kleipool, M. van Weele, O. Hasekamp, R. Hoogeveen, J. Landgraf, R. Snel, P. Tol, P. Ingmann, R. Voors, B. Kruizinga, R. Vink, H. Visser, P.F. Levelt, 2012: TROPOMI on the ESA Sentinel-5 Precursor: A GMES mission for global observations of the atmospheric composition for climate, air quality and ozone layer applications. Remote Sensing of Environment, Vol. 120, 15 May 2012, Pages 70-83, ISSN 0034-4257, 10.1016/j.rse.2011.09.027.

Vijayaraghavan, K., Snell, H., Seigneur, C., 2007: Feasibility of Using Satellite Data in Air Quality Modeling. CRC Report No. A-61, Coordinating Research Council, Inc., Alpharetta, GA, June 2007.

Wahlin, P., F. Palmgren and R. Van Dingenen, 2001: Experimental studies of ultrafine particles in streets and the relationship to traffic. Atmos. Environ., 35, S63–S69.

Wang, S., D.G. Streets, Q. Zhang, K. He, D. Chen, S. Kang, Z. Lu, and Y. Wang, 2010: Satellite detection and model verification of NOx emissions from power plants in Northern China. Environ. Res. Lett. 5, 044007.

West, J.J., A. M. Fiore, V. Naik, L. W. Horowitz, M.D. Schwarzkopf and D. L. Mauzerall, 2007: Ozone air quality and radiative forcing consequences of changes in ozone precursor emissions. Geophysical Research Letters, Vol. 34, L06806, doi:10.1029/2006GL029173.

Zhou, X., K. Civerolo, H. Dai, G. Huang, J. Schwab and K. Demerjian, 2002: Summertime nitrous acid chemistry in the atmospheric boundary layer at a rural site in New York State. J. Geophys. Res, 107, 10.1029/2001JD00153971.

Zhu, Y., Hinds, W.C., Kim, S and Sioutas, C., 2002: Concentration and Size Distribution of Ultrafine Particles near a Major Highway. J. Air & Waste Manage. Assoc., 52, 1032-10.

Introduction to Appendices for Existing Air Quality Monitoring Programs

Observation programs supporting air quality and related assessments include routine regulatory networks, deposition networks, intensive field studies, remote sensing systems, sondes, aircraft campaigns, satellites, and focused fixed-site special purpose networks. Appendices A – I provide information on a wide variety of these air monitoring networks. Major networks that are currently operating are emphasized; in some cases, reference to other networks that have been discontinued or were intended only for a specific operating period is also provided. The focus is on networks located in the United States, but attention is also given to other North American, European, and international efforts that contribute to U.S. assessments.

Information on monitoring networks represents the recent status of these networks (in terms of monitor number, placement, and measurement parameters). The actual status will likely have changed as of the publication date of this report for at least some of these networks as they expand or contract, consistent with current needs. For latest information on the status of many air quality monitoring networks, readers should consult AirData at http://www.epa.gov/airdata/ad_maps.html. Alternately, website links (which also periodically change) in these appendices should be consulted for the latest information on networks.

This information is the product of extensive Internet searches and information provided by knowledgeable representatives from the agencies responsible for the networks. In most cases, the information provided has been taken directly from the referenced Internet site, especially for supplemental information for the non-routine special intensive studies. Attribution of this information should be to those Internet websites.

Appendix A. Integrated Observational Strategies

Intensive field campaigns and observations from space provide valuable measurements not captured in routine, ground-based observation networks and can have direct impacts on the air quality management process. For example, results from the Texas Air Quality Study were incorporated into the ozone State Implementation Plan for the Houston area within two years. Similarly, satellite observations have played important roles in improving the quality of fire-based emissions estimates in EPA's systems for driving air quality models. And in the absence of an adequate surface-based network, satellite observations have been used to demonstrate the progress of major national programs to reduce emissions of nitrogen oxides.

Integrating these various types of observations with one another and with models to produce the best multi-dimensional characterization of air quality is a significant scientific and information-technology challenge, even in a research setting. Integration for decision-support purposes, near-real-time forecasting applications, and other operational purposes is even more challenging.

Over the last several years, a number of observational strategies and umbrella organizations have formed that convey and promote integration across disciplines, observational modalities, and/or organizations. Some of these efforts are focused on air quality or atmospheric chemistry, while some are far broader. These strategies and organizations include:

USGEO and GEO – The U.S. Group on Earth Observations (USGEO) exists as a subcommittee of the NSTC Committee on Environment, Natural Resources, and Sustainability (CENRS). USGEO's mandate is to: (1) coordinate, plan, and assess Federal Earth observation activities in cooperation with domestic stakeholders; (2) foster improved Earth system data management and interoperability throughout the Federal Government; and (3) engage international stakeholders by formulating the U.S. position for, and coordinating U.S. participation in, the intergovernmental GEO based in Geneva, Switzerland. GEO, a voluntary partnership of national governments and international organizations, is developing the Global Earth Observation System of Systems (GEOSS). GEOSS provides a voluntary, multidisciplinary framework to make all types of Earth observations more discoverable, accessible, and useable for decision support. In October 2010, Congress charged OSTP with a new "mechanism *to ensure greater coordination of the research, operations, and activities relating to civilian Earth observation*" [emphasis added] that would also produce and routinely update the strategic plan for Earth observations.[1] In response, OSTP developed and released a U.S. National Strategy in April 2013 and concurrently performed an internal assessment of 362 Federal Earth observing systems.

---

[1] National Aeronautics and Space Administration Authorization Act of 2010 (Public Law 111–267), § 703 "Interagency Collaboration Implementation Approach."

Summary results of this assessment will form the foundation for a new U.S. National Plan for Civil Earth Observations, to be published in 2014. This air quality observations report, along with other reports of the NSTC and the National Academies, provides important technical input to the development of the National Plan.

IGAC / AC&C – The International Global Atmospheric Chemistry (IGAC: http://www.igacproject.org/) program was created in the late 1980s to address growing international concern about atmospheric changes. IGAC is jointly sponsored by the Commission on Atmospheric Chemistry and Global Pollution (CACGP) of the International Association of Meteorology and Atmospheric Sciences (IAMAS) and the International Geosphere-Biosphere Programme (IGBP). IGAC has initiated or coordinated much of the research over the last decade focusing on chemical composition, transformations, and transport in the troposphere. Together with the Stratospheric Processes And their Role in Climate (SPARC) project of the World Climate Research Programme (WCRP), IGAC has started the Atmospheric Chemistry and Climate (AC&C; http://www.igacproject.org/node/8/) initiative, which examines the interplay between chemistry, chemically-active species, and climate change.

IGACO – Integrated Global Atmospheric Chemistry Observations (IGACO; http://www.igaco-o3.fi) is a strategy for bringing together ground-based aircraft and satellite observations of 13 chemical species in the atmosphere. IGACO will be implemented as a strategic element of the Global Atmospheric Watch (GAW) program of the World Meteorological Organization (WMO). IGACO will be organized around four focus areas, one of which is air quality / long-range transport. IGACO provides specific recommendations on measurement parameters, and facilitates integration across satellite- and ground-based stations. Although IGACO is focused on large, global-scale characterizations, the strategy provides useful guidance that should be considered in any air-based observation program design. Several of the core IGACO measurement parameters (O_3, CO, NO_2, and CO_2) are important regional- and urban-scale air quality indicators.

MACC – Monitoring Atmospheric Composition and Climate (MACC; http://www.gmes.info/pages-principales/projects/atmosphere-projects/macc/) is a recently initiated collaborative effort, funded by the European Commission, to monitor the global distribution and long-range transport of long-lived greenhouse gases, aerosols, and reactive pollutants that degrade air quality. MACC's product lines include data records on atmospheric composition for recent years, and current data for monitoring present conditions and forecasting the distribution of key constituents a few days ahead. (MACC is a continuation of the Global and regional Earth-system (Atmosphere) Monitoring using Satellite and in-situ data (GEMS) and PROtocol MOniToring for the GMES Service Element: Atmosphere (PROMOTE) programs under Global Monitoring for Environment and Security (GMES), see above website for details.)

NARSTO – NARSTO (formerly the North American Research Strategy for Tropospheric Ozone; http://www.narsto.org/) is a public-private partnership of government agencies, industry, and academic institutions. The partnership sponsors a variety of workshops and assessments addressing current air quality research interests. NARSTO has focused on the atmospheric sciences, with assessments addressing ozone and particulate matter air pollution, emissions inventories, and, more recently, multiple-pollutant air quality management. These assessments generally complement preceding NAS studies addressing air pollution management. The NARSTO archive stores data from a variety of intensive field campaigns.

NAAMS – The National Ambient Air Monitoring Strategy (NAAMS; http://www.epa.gov/ttnamti1/monitor.html) was developed jointly by the EPA and numerous state and local agencies. Developed in the early 2000s, NAAMS (Scheffe et al., 2009) was intended to make the design of U.S. regulatory-based networks more efficient in supporting the development of air quality standards and emission control strategies. The multi-pollutant National Core network (NCore, see Section 2) emerged from the NAAMS process.

AQAST – Air Quality Applied Sciences Team (AQAST; http://acmg.seas.harvard.edu/aqast/index.html) is a NASA team of atmospheric scientists working in partnership with U.S. air quality managers from local to national levels. The goal is to exploit the power of Earth science tools and data sets, available from NASA and other agencies, to address multi-faceted air quality problems. A wide range of projects using satellite data, suborbital data, and models are conducted through pooled expertise under the program.

Appendix B. Evolution of United States Air Monitoring Networks

The 1970 Clean Air Act (CAA) established a framework for the original National Ambient Air Quality Standards (NAAQS), and drove the design and implementation of the NAMS and SLAMS networks in the late 1970s. These networks were intended primarily to establish non-attainment areas with respect to the NAAQS, which include ozone, sulfur dioxide, nitrogen dioxide, carbon dioxide, lead (Pb), and particulate matter (PM). The NAMS/SLAMS networks have evolved over time (Figure A.1) as a result of cyclical NAAQS review and promulgation efforts, leading to changes in measurement requirements related to averaging times, locations, and the various size cuts associated with PM.

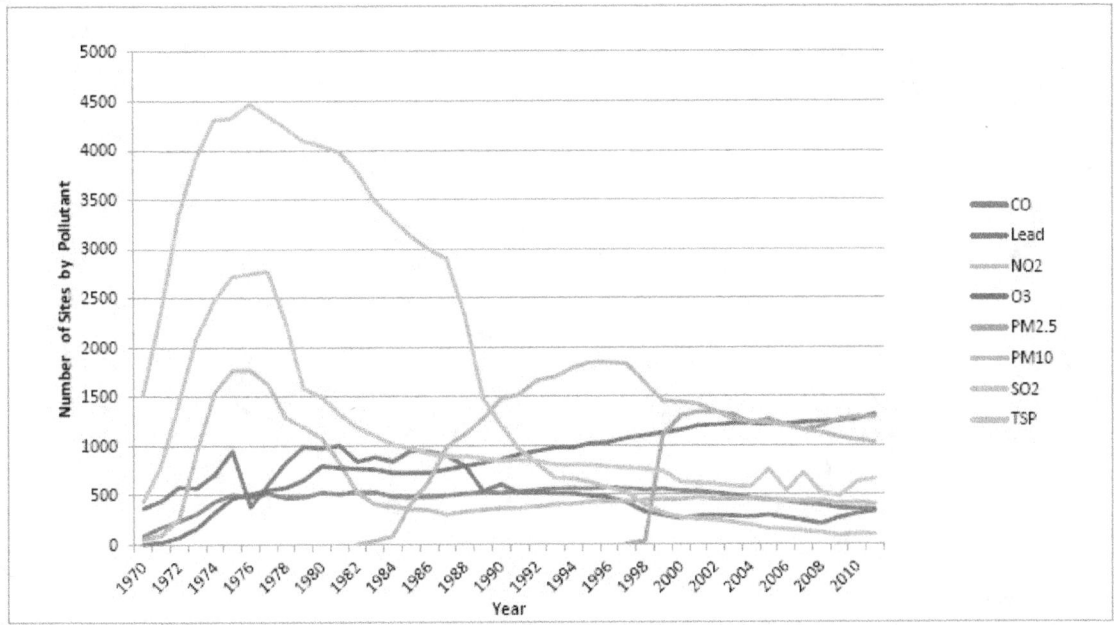

Figure B.1. Evolution of U.S. air network growth.

Relatively wide geographical distribution and persistence of ozone and PM$_{2.5}$ NAAQS exceedances (Figure A.2) have led to these pollutants dominating the national monitoring landscape.

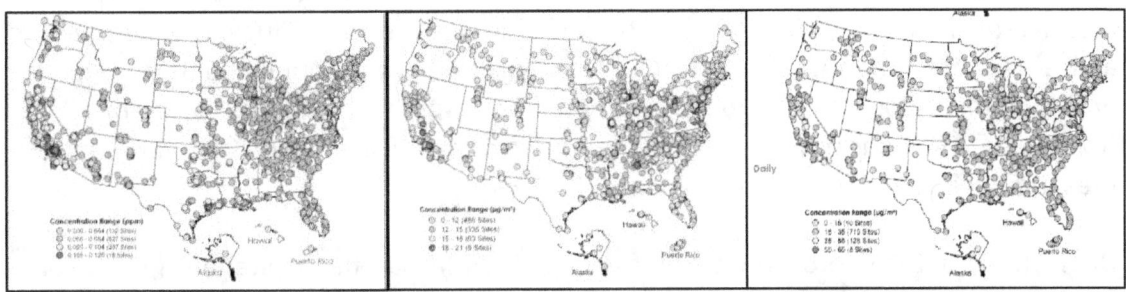

Figure B.2. 2006 air quality summaries for ozone, annual average PM$_{2.5}$, and daily PM$_{2.5}$.

Yellow and red sites indicate values exceeding NAAQS levels (source, EPA).
Two important ambient air networks focused on environmental welfare effects were
established in the mid -1980's. The Interagency Agency Monitoring of Protected Visual
Environments (IMPROVE) network consists of 212 sites (170 current and 42
discontinued) representing 156 visibility-protected federal areas (national parks,
wilderness areas, and wildlife refuges). IMPROVE is used primarily to assess visibility
impairment, but has provided a reliable long term record of PM mass and major
speciation components. It served as a model for the later deployment of EPA's CSN
network (Figure 2 of the full report), which has provided an urban complement to
characterize aerosol composition (Figure A.3).

**Figure B.3. Regional chemical composition of PM$_{2.5}$ aerosols -- composition of PM$_{2.5}$ for 15
selected urban areas in the United States. Annual average PM$_{2.5}$ concentrations (ug/m^3) are
presented, the circle size representing the magnitude of PM$_{2.5}$ mass.**

The Clean Air Status and Trends Network (CASTNET) was established in the early 1990s
to track changes in dry deposition of major inorganic ions and gaseous precursors
associated with the CAA Title 4 reductions in sulfur and nitrogen. Title 4 was designed to
address surface water acidification in eastern North America. Complementing ongoing
precipitation measurements from the National Atmospheric Deposition Program
(NADP), CASTNET has provided a valuable source of model evaluation data for many of
the large regional scale applications since the 1990's.

Deployment of the Photochemical Assessment and Measurements Stations (PAMS) and
the PM$_{2.5}$ networks from the early 1990's through 2002 markedly enhanced the spatial,
temporal, and compositional measurement of gases and aerosols. PAMS partially
supports user needs beyond NAAQS compliance, such as public reporting and

forecasting of adverse air quality, implementation efforts including air quality model evaluation, and source apportionment and pattern (spatial and temporal) analysis of precursor species.

State and local air agencies have measured a variety of metallic and gaseous hazardous air pollutants (HAPs) at over 200 locations since the 1980's. Typically, broad access to and use of data was compromised by a lack of centralized databases and multiple sampling and laboratory protocols leading to data uncertainty. In response to this gap in accessible and centralized HAPs observations, a modest 27 site National Air Toxics Trends (NATTS) network was initiated in 2001. Current NATTS species include: acrolein, perchloroethylene, benzene, carbon tetrachloride, chloroform, trichloroethylene, 1,3-butadiene, 1,2-dichloropropane, dichloromethane, tetrachloroethylene, vinyl chloride, formaldehyde, acetaldehyde, nickel compounds, arsenic compounds, cadmium compounds, manganese compounds, beryllium, lead, hexavalent chromium, and expected additions of benzo(a)pyrene and naphthalene.

A new multi-pollutant monitoring network, referred to as NCore, was incorporated in the 2006 revisions to the particulate matter standards. When fully implemented, NCore will provide a minimum of 75 Level 2 sites (Figure A.4) in most major urban areas and important transport corridor and background locations. NCore will include a variety of trace gas, aerosol mass and speciation measurements which are intended to support multiple data user needs (e.g., air quality model evaluation, long term epidemiological studies). In addition to establishing a multiple pollutant measurement framework, the NCore sites are intended to provide a backbone of central location sites that can be complemented by additional (existing and new) stations to address more specific spatial resolution requirements. Intensive Level 1 sites, intended to promote transition of new technologies into routine networks, have not been implemented to date.

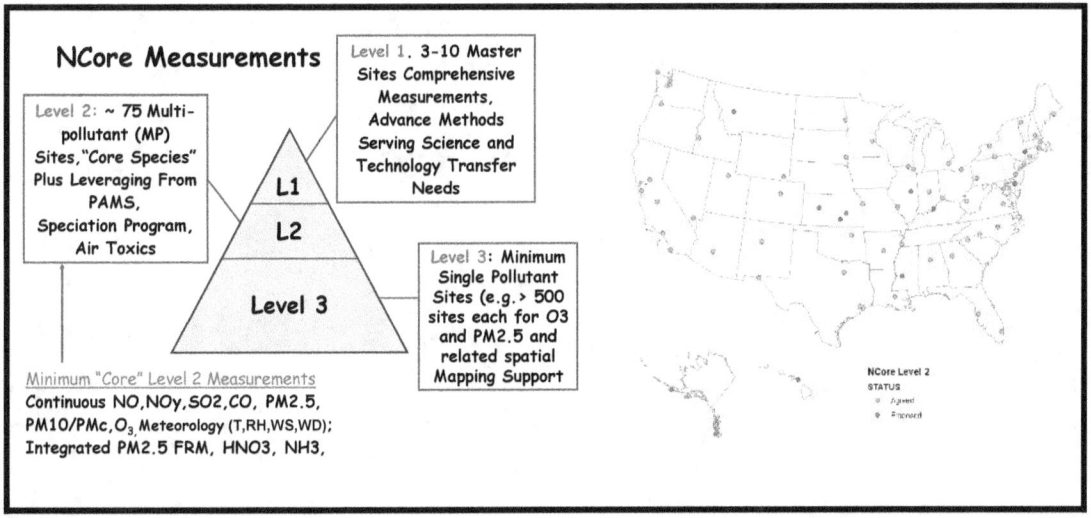

Figure B.4. Original 3-tiered NCore design (left) and proposed site locations (see http://www.epa.gov/ttn/amtic/ncore/networks.html for updated site locations)